History
(and other things)
Reconsidered

Author of

Space-Time (and other things) Reconsidered

History
(and other things)
Reconsidered

Essays Reconsidering History and
Commentary on How Progressive Agendas
Affect Contemporary Writings on History...

John H. Silver

Beagle Publishing
2018

Copyright © 2018 by John H. Silver

All rights reserved. This book or any part thereof may not be reproduced or used in any manner whatsoever without the express written permission of the publisher except for the use of brief quotations in a book review or scholarly journal.

ISBN: **978-1987622546**

Cover Photo:
Litte Bighorn Battle Field National Monument
Author's photograph taken at the Reno-Benteen site. Foreground: Markers for three fallen army scouts. Background: ravine to the Little Bighorn River.

Beagle Publishing

Printed by CreateSpace

Contents

Preface ix
Part 1: Essays Reconsidering History 1
Part 1 Introduction 1

1.1   The First 100 Years.................................. 3
Introduction 3
Christianity: The First 100 Years..5
   Beginnings 5
   Apostolic Period (30 – 100) 6
      Years 30 - 59...6
      Paul of Tarsus..7
      Years 60 - 69...8
      Years 70 - 100...9
   Post Apostolic Period (100 to 132) 11
Final Comments 12
Islam: The First 100 Years 15
   Beginnings 15
   The Rashidun Caliphs (632 – 661)................................19
   Umayyad Dynasty (661 to 732) 22
Final Comments 24
Coda...26

1.2   The Conquest of Mexico 29
   Cast of Characters..29
Introduction 30
The Background 31
   The Mexica 31
   The Spanish 32
The Conquest..33
   The Arrival 33
   The Advance Inland 34
   The Cholula Incident...34
   The Arrival in Tenochtitlan 35
   The Narvaez Incident..36
   The Night of Sorrows 37
   The Recovery and Preparation 39
   The Fall of Tenochtitlan 39
Recapitulation: How Cortes Won.....................................41
Appendix: Conquest versus Colonizing..........................46

1.3   The First Thirty Years War: 1618-1648........ 49
Introduction 49
Major Phases of the War 53
   Bohemian Conflict (1618-1625) 53
   Danish Intervention (1625-1629)..................................54
   Swedish Intervention (1630-1635) 55

  French Intervention (1635-1648) 56
  Peace of Westphalia (1648) 56
The War's Legacy 58

1.4 Custer's Last Battle 61
Preface 61
Background: Custer at the Washita 62
Considering the Battle 64
Reconsidering the Battle 66
  The Plan: June 1876 66
  Crook Meets the Unexpected 67
  The First Day: June 22, 1876 68
  The Second Day: June 23, 1876 69
  The Third Day: 0500 June 24 - 1200 June 25th 69
The Last Hours: June 25 - 1200 to 2100 73
  The First Big Mistake 73
  The Second Big Mistake 75
  First Contact: 1500 to 1610 Hours 76
  Comments on Artifacts and Testimonies 80
  Custer's actions from 1530 to 1730 June 25th 81
  June 25th: Reno Hill - 1725 to 2100 Hours 83
  June 26: The Next Day at Reno Hill 84
Recapitulation 86
  Coda: The 400-Year War 90
Appendix: Custer's Orders from General Terry 91
Attachments 92

1.5 The Second Thirty Years War: 1914 - 1945 ... 97
Introduction 97
Preparing for the Storm 99
General Mobilization 101
Stalemate: 1914 – 1916 102
  Two Battles 103
   Verdun: February 1916 – December 1916 103
   Somme July 1916 – November 1916 103
The Turn of the Tide: 1917 - 1918 105
The Treaty of Versailles 108
  French Issues 108
  British Issues 109
  American Issues 109
  German Issues 110
  Japanese Issues 111
  Fallout from the Treaty 111
Germany 1919 - 1933 113
  Weimar Republic 113
  National Socialism on the Rise 114
World War II Starts in Asia: 1931 115
  The Manchurian Incident 115
The Third Reich: 1933 – 1939 116

- Hitler Becomes Chancellor 116
- Hitler Becomes Dictator 116
- Rearmament and Land Grabs 117

Start of Aggressive War: 1939 - 1945 119
- Blitzkrieg Tested on Poland 119
- Hitler Moves North 119
- Blitzkrieg in the West 119
- Taking on the Colossus 121
- Turn of the Tide 121
- Closing the Ring 122
- Hitler's Gamble in the West 123
- Spring Thaw in the West 124
- The War in Asia 125

Was Use of the Atom Bombs Justified? 127
Aftermath 128
- Changes: 1945 and Beyond 128

Coda 131

Part 2: Commentary on Contemporary Historical Writings 133

2.1 Miscellany of Preliminary Topics 135
- Judgments (hasty and otherwise) 135
- Sufficient Evidence for Belief 136
- Language 139
- Explanations and Perception 140
- Symbolic versus Intimate Knowledge 142
- Sensory Pollution 143
- Sensitivity? 145
- Too Much Technology? 145
- The Unexpected 147
- Cause and Effect 148
- Dynamic Accommodation 149
- Intersubjective Agreement 149
- Groupthink 150
- Truth and Validity 152

2.2 Contemporary History: A Commentary 153
Reconsidering Reality 154
- Types of Reality 155

Influences on Contemporary History 159
- Sources and Veracity of Information 159
- Information Deprivation 161
- Testimonial Injustice 164
- Tolerance and Free Speech 165
- Tyranny of Imposition 166
- Social Epistemology 168
- Social Constructionism 171
- Summary 173

Revisionist History and Contextual Displacement 175
Appendix A: Reconsidering Global Warming 179

    Computer Simulations and Modeling 179
    Global Climate Discussion 180
Selected Bibliography 183
General Index 184

Preface

History is a fragile subject. It is easily modified by omission, interpretation, selective content, and selective emphasis. Since human events always have multiple points of view, it is probable that pure objectivity in historical interpretations cannot be obtained. Of course, writing on history is only one example of a condition that holds true for all human actions and interactions, there is always a subjective element.

Part 1 is a diverse selection of short essays that discuss historical events that have been written about and discussed many times and will continue to be written about in the future.

The choice of topics for these essays was partly based on prior interest or were suggested to me by contemporary events and social attitudes. The essay on Custer is an example of the first kind, while the essay on the historical beginnings of Christianity and Islam is an example of the second kind.

Although, the subjects of these essays vary considerably, they all have the common problem of frequent, intentional or un-intentional, misrepresented. Therefore, my goal has been to present these topics as objectively as possible, while offering some new explanations and insights.

Part 2 begins with a miscellany of topics that are relevant to the following discussion on contemporary historiography and the social factors that are influencing writing on history in particular, and society, in general. That is, what is now become prevalent in historical commentaries, has also become prevalent within our society.

John H. Silver
April 2018
Santa Rosa, CA
jhslbc@gmail.com

x

Part 1: Essays Reconsidering History

Part 1 Introduction

History is an indispensable tool in helping us understand our world and how we got to where we are today. History also plays a role in the formation of our personal and social worldviews and cultural identification. All earthly societies that advanced beyond the hunter-gatherer stages developed written language and maintained historical records of various kinds.

The value of these records, written hundreds or even thousands of years in the past, cannot be overstated, they are our primary window into the past, but being the work of humans, they are susceptible to human error and bias.[1]

When these historical records are commentaries, they have agendas, public and hidden, that are always present in some form, either tacitly or overtly. In either case, they await the historian who has the task of uncovering these agendas and presenting their own interpretations and explanations of these records with an open mind and a minimum of personal agenda.

However, no matter how hard a person might try, no one is completely objective, there is always a subjective influence motivated either consciously or unconsciously by personal agendas and prejudices (Yes, we all have them).

On the other hand, there are those individuals who purposely instill subjectivity such as personal or social agendas into their historical writings, and then pass them off as being objective and truthful. That is, these writers will modify or selectively filter opinions to support their biases and agendas.

This is especially true when strong emotional issues are considered. For example, we see this regularly when an issue becomes politicized such that logic, rationality, and even truth become secondary to political agendas.

---

[1] Written records used by historians include primary sources such as letters, legal documents, and first-hand accounts, while secondary sources include such documents as other historical works and non-eyewitness accounts.

Some of these writings have, over the past few decades, had an unfortunate amount of influence on history in general, and US history, in particular. These writings offer a negative revisionist point of view.

Of course, sometimes, the opposite is true, and historical presentations are modified in order not to blame, but to remove blame or, perhaps, just to show bias and favoritism regarding certain historical events, individuals, or groups.

In attempting to avoid either extreme, what I have strived in these essays is to be as objective as possible by avoiding omissions or modifications based on personal bias, present a balanced historical commentary, and minimize subjectivity.

Notice, I said minimize, because I do not believe anyone can truly eliminate subjectivity completely. The goal has been to present the circumstances of these events in a manner that allows the reader to reach their own conclusions and, hopefully, to provide an interesting and unique narrative concerning the selected topics.

1.1 The First 100 Years

Reconsidering the Historical Beginnings of Christianity and Islam…

Introduction

Between them, Christianity and Islam statistically account for more than 50% of the world's population. Even though, these two religions have co-existed for almost 1400 years, until the 20th century, these two religions had little contact with each other except where they either coincided (Egypt) or had common frontiers (the Balkans).

Even today, when there is more cross exposure between these two religions, most Christians know little about Islam and the same can be said about knowledge of Christianity among most Muslims. This lack of knowledge, along with the increased tensions between the followers of these religions, means that each tends to regard the other with suspicion, misunderstanding, and myth.

This essay is intended as a modest step in helping bridge the lack of understanding, and what better way than to start at the beginnings of both religions. Each had very different beginnings, but within one hundred years, both were firmly implanted in their specific spheres of influence, which, as will be shown, coincided to a considerable degree.

This essay is *not a review of doctrines or beliefs* held by these religions, rather the content is historical in the sense that discussion is about the social, political, and geographical, not the theological or doctrinal.

Having said that, I must add that complete avoidance of theology or doctrine is not possible because of the overlap of the spiritual with the secular. This is especially true of Islam where both the spiritual and the secular have always been connected and are inseparable.

Perhaps, because Christianity pre-dates Islam by almost exactly 600 years, there is less variety in the primary sources of information for the early years of Christianity than those existing about early Islam. For the most part, the New testament is the source of information on the early years of Christianity.

On the other hand, secondary sources for both religions were mostly written years after the events discussed and consequently may or may not be completely valid. There is also the problem of precisely dating when events occurred. Different authors, sometimes, use different dates and all that can be done is pick the one that seems most frequently used or that seems most reasonable.

However, whatever the veracity or variety of documentation, I have tried to present the facts as closely as they can be determined, and since primary and secondary sources for both were written in antiquity and essentially beyond possible verification, the sources for both religions are not judged for accuracy.

Christianity is discussed first because of age, not any priority.

Christianity: The First 100 Years

Beginnings

Here in the West, the story of the birth and life of Jesus is well known and need not be repeated in any detail. Therefore, only three events in his life will be recalled.

The first event is his baptism by John the Baptist. It is significant that John referred to Jesus as the *Lamb of God*, which at that time was the traditional Jewish sacrificial animal. Apparently, this usage was a reference to Jesus' eventual fate of prophesized martyrdom.

The second event, is the preaching known as the *Sermon on the Mount*. This sermon used direct speaking, which was different from most of his others that tended to use parables and proverbs. It is in the that part of the sermon known as the *Nine Beatitudes* (Matthew 5:3-12), where true uniqueness of his legacy lies. At that time, these nine were unlike anything ever put forward by any known religion, and they axiomatically defined early Christianity.

The third is the martyrdom and resurrection, thought to be in the year 30, which through the fulfillment of the prophesies firmly established his credibility and inspired his apostles to continue their missionary sanction.

Apostolic Period (30 - 100)

The years 30 to 100 is the span of years known as the Apostolic Period (or Age). This is the time when the original Apostles, along with the new apostles Paul and James the Just, a brother of Jesus, spread the teachings of Jesus throughout much of the known world, which at that time, mostly coincided with the Roman Empire.

Years 30 - 59

Following the crucifixion, the continued spread of Christianity depended on the Apostles to pick up where Jesus left off and start the fulfillment of his sanction that instructed the Apostles to spread the *Word* even unto the *ends of the earth*.

After a brief period of confusion, the Apostles soon started on their assigned or chosen missions and began extensive travel, which would take some of them to the *ends* of the known world, beyond the boundaries of the Roman Empire and into Ethiopia and India.

However, before spreading throughout the Roman Empire, the Apostles, along with James the Just, were mostly active in expanding their following within Jerusalem and the surrounding area. It is important to note, that during these first years after the crucifixion, only Jews were accepted as converts. These early converts, and the Apostles themselves, continued to follow traditional Jewish ritual augmented with the additional belief that Jesus was the Messiah. They were known as Jewish-Christians.

From the point of view of the Roman civil authorities in these early years, the Jewish-Christians were not differentiated from the rest of Jewry and therefore received the same treatment. Later, toward the end of the first century, they became recognized as a distinct religion, which might or might not have been an advantage. That would depend on the local attitude and who was emperor at the time.

The Roman Empire had long been dealing with the Jews, but the Christian variation of Judaism was new and as such was likely to cause some anxiety or, at least, some suspicion. This is the period when in some places, the church was literally underground, with the most famous example being the so-called Roman Catacombs.

After about twenty years of proselytizing among their fellow Jews, a significant event occurred. In the year 50, the leadership of Christianity, met in a council, later called the *Council of Jerusalem*, which after much debate, decided that non-Jews (gentiles) could be accepted as converts. This decision was made in large part due to the influence of the apostle Paul and was a significant event in the history of Christianity. It was only through the acceptance of gentiles that Christianity was able to expand and thrive. Essentially, this acceptance opened up Christianity for wide acceptance and saved the movement from being a minor Jewish sect, with limited chances of survival.

Paul of Tarsus

Although Paul (aka Saul of Tarsus) was converted in the year 32, it was not until the 40's that he began his missionary work and soon became a leader of the Christian movement second only to Peter, or, perhaps, the equal of Peter.[2] As a missionary, Paul had the advantage of being a Jew and a Roman citizen. Given his place of birth, the city of Tarsus (southwest Anatolia), it is likely that he was raised speaking both Greek and Hebrew.

In any case, in was in the 40's when he began his twenty-year sanction that was to, not only, expand Christianity geographically but he also seems to have defined Christianity theologically more than any of the original Apostles.

Paul, likely because of his origin in a Roman city he was worldlier than the other apostles, began early on to advocate the inclusion of non-Jews, or gentiles, as potential converts. This notion was at first controversial, because, at that time, Christianity was seen only as an extension of Judaism, and it was felt that only those who followed Judaism were worthy candidates for conversion. As mentioned above, it was not until the Council of Jerusalem, in the year 50, that the issue was resolved, and Paul was free to begin his missions to convert gentiles.[3]

It should be remembered, at this time, being a gentile meant being a polytheistic pagan. The advantage was that they were probably easier to convert than the Jews who were tightly bound to their theology. More importantly, the inclusion of gentiles opened the door for a far greater expansion than would have been possible if the restriction to Judaism had remained in effect.

---

[2] Most scholars agree that Peter, Paul, and James the Just were the leaders of the apostles, or, at least, the most influential.

[3] Paul is sometimes referred to as *The Apostle to the Gentiles*.

After the year 50, Paul's sanction took him as far as Iberia, although his main efforts were mostly within the Roman Hellenistic provinces, Syria, and, finally, about the year 60, Rome.

Besides his travels, Paul was also a prolific writer and wrote many letters (epistles). These letters served as a means of spreading the messages of Christianity without traveling, and by copying, they provided a means of reaching more people. These letters were essentially intended to be read aloud as sermons.[4]

Since his letters comprised 14 of the 27 books of the New Testament, the importance of these letters is clear. They, essentially, form the backbone of the New Testament.[5] It is these letters, more than any others that define Christianity as originally envisioned. It seems apparent that the influence of Paul far outreaches the influence of any other of the original Apostles, even Peter.

Years 60 - 69

It is somewhat remarkable, that by the early 60's, even with the obstacles presented by hostilities and open persecutions, the apostles were able to spread Christianity's message throughout much of the Roman Empire and beyond. Although, by this time, gentiles were being converted, the enclaves of Christianity were still mostly within Jewish settlements scattered throughout the Roman Empire.

For example, by this time there were enclaves in Rome (Peter and Paul), Egypt-Ethiopia (Mark), Iberia (James), and even India (Thomas). It is not surprising, that as Judaism was scattered in urban enclaves throughout the Empire, so to was early Christianity scattered. There were also enclaves throughout the Levant, including the city of Antioch, where it is thought that the term Christian, meaning followers of Jesus, was first used.

It was also about this time (the middle 60's) that there occurred several events that had an impact on the future development of Christianity. In

---

[4] It is believed that he used his extensive jail time to compose many of these letters.

[5] These fourteen are Paul's only known letters, however, there were probably others that were lost early on.

64, there was a great fire in Rome that was later blamed, by the Emperor Nero, on the Christians. This caused an increase in Christian persecution.

Possibly as a direct result of the increased persecution, it was also about this same time that the deaths of the two leading apostles, Peter and Paul, presumably occurred in Rome and by order of Nero. Unfortunately, the historical record is uncertain about when, where, and how these two apostles died.

The loss of these two apostles, along with increased persecution, must have had a severe impact on Christian morale, and likely caused the surviving apostles to take a more active leadership role. If things weren't bad enough, following these events, in 66, certain factions within Jerusalem revolted against Roman rule, and as with most revolts against Rome, this one was also destined to fail.

Years 70 - 100

The revolt in Jerusalem went on for several years, and it was not until after a lengthy siege that Jerusalem fell to the Romans. This occurred in the year 70, and was followed by the usual post-siege massacre, which was then followed by the complete destruction of the city.

With Jerusalem destroyed, the Jewish-Christians, along with the rest of the surviving population, were forced from Jerusalem and into exile. This dispersion (or Diaspora as it is often called) ushered in a period of about twenty years, where little is known about the state of Christianity and its expansion.

This dispersal from Jerusalem forced the apostles to look for a new center for their religion, and what better place than Rome. Additionally, the dispersal and lose of the center of Judaism made it even more necessary to seek converts elsewhere, and this of course meant more emphasis on proselytizing gentiles.

After the fall of Jerusalem, we do know that Christianity continued to spread into gentile communities such that gentiles soon became the dominant group of converts. It is not surprising that this shift to gentile dominance widened the gap between Judaism and Christianity, and before the end of the first century they had separated enough to be considered separate religions.

In any case, it is safe to assume that, given the age of even the youngest apostle, the original apostles were passing on and the next generation of church leaders and missionaries were continuing the missionary sanction. That is, by the year 70 and beyond, the efforts of the surviving Apostles were assisted and augmented by the next generation of leadership until the year 100. It is this year when the last of the original Apostles, John, died in Ephesus, and the transition to the next generation was complete.

Although Christianity continued to revere the Jewish Bible, confirmation of the split between the two occurred during the reign of the Emperor Nerva (96-98) when he modified the tax on Jews such that Christians did not have to pay the annual tax. Additional confirmation can be seen in a letter from Pliny the Younger (61-113) to the Emperor Trajan (98-117), Pliny mentioned that Christians were seen as separate from Jews. However, even so, Jewish-Christians were to be found in various communities for another two or three hundred years.

Post Apostolic Period (100 to 132)

By the year 100, the Christian faith was firmly established throughout the Mediterranean Basin and as far as Ethiopia and India. Although wide spread, there was, during these early years, no intention or notion of Christianity as a political instrument. The entire focus and motivation appears to have been conversion and salvation, with no political agenda, with the possible exception of being recognized as legitimate and free from persecution.

Given the wide geographic spread and diversity of cultures where Christianity had taken root, the development of some differences in belief and dogma is not surprising. Because of these differences, it was also this period that saw the beginnings of attempts to standardize Christianity and exclude beliefs considered inappropriate or possibly even heretical.

However, despite this effort, it would take several centuries before most of these diverse groups would either be dissolved or converted to more mainstream views. While these efforts were in progress, Christianity continued its expansion through rhetorical persuasion and voluntary conversion.

I chose to stop at the year 132, because it marks the start of the second revolt of the Jews against Roman rule. This time Jerusalem, completely depopulated and destroyed in 70, was rebuilt by the Emperor Hadrian as a pagan city of Rome, and was given the Latin name Aelia Capitolina. This symbolically and physically removed Christianity from Jerusalem until the Byzantines occupied the city in the early 4th century.

Final Comments

The development and spread of Christianity in the 2nd and 3rd centuries is both less studied and less documented than are later centuries. These two centuries, besides being referred to as the Post-Apostolic Period, are often called the ante-Nicene Period since they preceded the famous *Council of Nicaea*, which was held in 325.

Nevertheless, there were prominent leaders of the Post-Apostolic period, whose writings have survived. For example, notable among these early leaders were *Clement of Alexandria* (Egypt) and *Irenaeus of Lyons* (France), both of whom were active around the year 200. Clement wrote in Greek, while Irenaeus, Greek by birth, eventually relocated to France, where he wrote in Latin. The geographical dispersion of these two illustrate how the church had spread from east to west, and by the year 200 was moving north from the Mediterranean Basin into the heart of Europe.

The result, with minor exceptions, was a two-way split between the Latin speaking world of the West and the Greek speaking world of the East. The West became centered around the Bishop of Rome, while the East was less centrally controlled. The Eastern Orthodox evolved such that there were five Patriarchs, each essentially equal.[6]

As briefly mentioned above, eventually, and for many reasons, the church of the east and the church of the west gradually moved farther apart with regard to ritual and doctrine. This occurred for many reasons, but perhaps the most significant being the use of Latin in the West and Greek in the East. Although the eastern Patriarchs continued to respect the Bishop of Rome as having a special authority based on seniority, this authority was limited, and the Patriarchs held final authority in their respective patriarchates. The degree to which the west-east split had influence is clearly illustrated by the following event.

The *Nicene Creed*, first published in the year 325 following the above-mentioned *Council of Nicaea*, evolved over time and by the 15th century, the Western Catholic Church, and the Eastern Orthodox Church had different versions of this creed. The Catholic version contained the Latin word *filioque*, which translates as *and from the son*. The Orthodox Greek version of the creed did not contain this word.

---

[6] These early patriarchates were in Rome, Alexandria, Antioch, Jerusalem, and Byzantium (Constantinople).

Consequently, in an age of strong religious ardor, this difference was enough to cause a rift between these two branches of Christianity such that, in 1453, when Constantinople, the center of Eastern Orthodoxy, was under siege by the Ottoman Empire, the Christian West would not send aid to the Christian East. The result was the capture of Constantinople and the history of Europe and Asia were changed forever. Never underestimate the power of a single word!

As for Christianity, in general, it is fair to claim that for the first few hundred years, Christianity had no political agendas other than co-existence within the various communities where it was established. In fact, it is probably this lack of political agendas that enabled early Christianity to co-exist.

It was only after the adoption of Christianity by the Roman Empire in the 4th century that Christianity can be said to have moved from being concerned mostly with matters of the spirit and became involved with secular matters as well.[7]

However, even after becoming the state religion of Rome, there was no sudden shift into the affairs of government. As a side comment, it should be noted that, although a strong and respected moral influence, the eastern Orthodoxy remains even today mostly non-secular.

This acceptance as a state religion, put an end to persecutions, but with this acceptance came changes that moved the Church, slowly, at first, into an increasing secular role. As church leaders grew in wealth and status, the Roman church grew more secular and even, in some places, became an element or extension of government.[8] But all this took centuries to develop and it was not until the 16th century that church involvement in secular affairs peaked and helped spark the Reformation. But that is another story for another time.[9]

---

[7] The first country to adopt Christianity as the official state religion was Armenia. This occurred around the year 301, more than 20 years before the Roman Empire under Constantine adopted Christianity.

[8] For example, in England, bishops of the Church of England are still members of the House of Lords.

[9] Much of the Church's wealth came from land holdings. For example, by the time of the Reformation in England, the Church held about one third of all the land in England!

The First 100 Years

Islam: The First 100 Years

Beginnings

Muhammad was born in Mecca in the year 570. At that time, and for centuries prior, Mecca had been a center for caravan trade, as well as a place of religious pilgrimage.

It was a place of trade, because it was a crossroad on the trade routes from Yemen to the south, Persia to the east, Syria to the north, and Egypt to the west.

It was a place of pilgrimage because of an ancient temple centered around a large black stone called the Kaaba. Although, this temple contained images of more than 300 deities, the black stone represented a deity superior to all the others.

Both the caravans and the pilgrimages brought in a steady stream of visitors from all over Arabia as well as those from more distant regions. These visitors provided excellent opportunities for the exchange of ideas, which surely would have included a multitude of diverse religious beliefs, which would have included Jewish and Christian doctrine, as well as the many pagan beliefs of the dessert tribes.

The time of the pilgrimages was a time of truce and no violence was allowed in Mecca at those times, and some say that, as a holy city, violence was forbidden in Mecca at all times. In any case, the pilgrimages provided an influx of considerable commerce that made many Meccan's wealthy.

The main recipients of this wealth were the Quraysh tribe, which was not only the ruling tribe of Mecca, this tribe also claimed to have descended from the ancient prophets, Abraham and Ishmael.[10]

Although, little is known for certain about Muhammad's early life. he was apparently a member of the Hashemite clan that was part of the ruling Quraysh tribe. Of these early years, it is said that when Muhammad was

---

[10] The people of Arabia, like so many other ancient cultures, was based on family, clan, and tribal affiliations, which formed the hierarchy of loyalty and precedence. Even today there are cultures where any social affiliations beyond tribal are only loosely held.

about 12, he traveled with his uncle's caravan to Syria, and while on this trip, he encountered a Christian monk named Bahira.

As the story goes, the monk spoke of a prophecy that a great prophet would someday pass his way. After speaking with Muhammad, Bahira declared that Muhammad would become this prophet. Another version is a little different and says that Muhammad made more than one trip to Syria, and that Muhammad and Bahira had many conversations. In any case, speculation is that it was Bahira who instilled Muhammad with the belief in one God by teaching Muhammad about Judaism and Christianity.

However, that may be, it is known that at the age of 25, Muhammad married a wealthy widow who had been his employer. Her name is given as Khadija and she operated the caravans of her late husband that traded with both Syria to the north and Yemen to the south. This marriage elevated Muhammad's social status and improved his standard of living. This improved lifestyle, apparently, gave Muhammad time to ponder matters other than the prosaic needs of everyday life.

Whether the story of Bahira is true or not, knowledge of Judaism and Christianity would have been easy to acquire because of the numerous caravans that passed through Mecca. Regardless of where or when he obtained his knowledge of Judaism and Christianity, he did not start his mission until 610, when he was 40 years old. Exactly how spent the 15 years between his marriage and the beginning of his mission as a prophet little is known.

Apparently, he spent much time alone in the desert, and it is here that he began to receive visions from the Archangel Gabriel. He claimed that these visions told him that, in a line from Abraham through Moses to Jesus, there would be one last great prophet of the one God, and that Muhammad was sanctioned to be that prophet.

Without going into details of his activities from 610 until his death in 632, Muhammad was able to build his vision from only a handful of converts within his family and close associates to a full blow religious movement spread across all of Arabia. Unfortunately, exactly how he was able to accomplish this feat is not known in great detail.

For the sake of brevity, only three events during the 22-year period from 610 to his death in 632 will be mentioned.

First, is his flight from Mecca to Medina in 622, known as the *Hegira*. After several years having little success in Mecca as a prophet, somehow, he managed to appeal to the citizens of a town north of Mecca that, although pagan, this town also happened to have a large Jewish enclave, and it is likely that the notion of one God was well known within this community. However, how and why this came about is somewhat vague, but it seems that the citizens invited Muhammad and his followers to move to their city, which later was renamed Medina (City of the Prophet).

Anyway, after barely escaping from a murder plot hatched by some citizens of Mecca, Muhammad and his small band of followers migrated to this town. After establishing himself in the town, he found that he now had, in addition to his role as spiritual leader, a secular role. This appealed to Muhammad and he was able to merge his spiritual role with his newly found secular role.

This was the first step in the process that eventually made Islam a religion where the secular and the spiritual are inextricably joined under *Islamic Law*. The significance of this flight to Medina is commemorated by the Islamic calendar where year one is the year of the flight.

Second, is the shift from preaching and gathering converts to aggressive action against both those he considered his enemies, as well as those he wished to convert. This change fit well into the Bedouin tradition, of which he was a part by culture and lineage.

For the Bedouin, religion and war are intertwined, such that they are not only compatible, but were an integral part of life. Life in the vast deserts of Arabia was difficult and open conflicts between tribes or even between clans of the same tribe were considered normal and necessary.

In 624, just two years after the flight to Medina, Muhamad fights his first battle, which happened to be against his Meccan foes, and was able to claim his first victory.[11] Although it wasn't much of a fight, it was enough to convinced Muhammad that he had real power.

After this initial success, he came to see aggressive warfare as the means of spreading his beliefs not only throughout Arabia, but the rest of the

---

[11] Battle of Badr.

world as well. This was big planning for a religion that was still limited to the deserts of Arabia.

Third, after his victory at the Battle of Badr, he was able to consolidate his position in Medina, which included the massacre of most of the Jews in that city, who had protested his policies. In any case, by 629, Muhammad's status as both prophet and secular leader were enhanced enough such that he was able to return to Mecca in triumphant. He was able to make a deal with the leaders of Mecca, which included making Mecca, and the Kaaba temple, in particular, the center of his religion.

This agreement required the destruction of all idols within the Kaaba, with the exception of the Kaaba stone, which would now be an Islamic relic and would continue to be an object of worship. This essentially meant that Mecca, as the center of Islam, would continue to be a place of pilgrimage. This agreement attenuated the hostility toward Muhammad by appeasing the Quraysh tribal leaders since they would continue to profit from pilgrimages.

In June of 632, Muhammad became ill and was taken to the house of his wife, Aisha. There he died on the 8th day of June and was buried within Aisha's house.

The Rashidun Caliphs (632 - 661)

In 632, only three years after his return to Mecca, Muhammad died, and his longtime friend and convert, Abu Bakr, was chosen to be the first Caliph.[12] Although not of direct blood line as Muhammad, and already old, he must have seemed the best choice, even though it left out a more natural selection of Muhammad's son-in-law and nephew, Ali ibn Abi Talib, whose father, Abi Talib, was one of Muhammad's first converts and uncle.

As the first Caliph, Abu found himself in a novel situation that had not been planned by Muhammad. That is, Muhammad had not made any arrangements for a successor. The concept of Caliphate was new and not well defined, but it provided Abu with a path for succession as both the legitimate spiritual and secular leader of Islam. Of course, without a precedence, Abu would have needed to improvise and define what it meant to be the Caliph.

However, first, he had to quell the apostate rebellion of some tribes of Arabia, who had after the death of Muhammad stopped paying tribute and were turning back to the old ways.

Remarkably, within a relatively brief time, Abu was able to bring the tribes of Arabia back into line, however, in 634, after only two years as Caliph, he died. Abu must have been a person of exceptional skill, because during that brief time, he was also able, to begin the expansion of Islam outside of the Arabia peninsula into Syria and Iraq. This was the beginning of the almost irresistible expansion of Islam for the next two decades.

Following the death of Abu, Ali was again passed by, and it was Umar, brother-in-law of the prophet, who became the second Caliph, and it was his ten years as Caliph that was primarily responsible for the first great expansion of Islam. By the time of his death, in 644, he expanded Islam by conquest north into the Levant (Syria, Jordan, Lebanon, Israel), west into Egypt, and east into the Sasanian Persian Empire (Iraq and Iran)

It should be noted, that after the fall of Rome in the 5th century, the former western Roman provinces broke up into petty kingdoms and principalities whose governments, lacking the skill and firm hand of

---

[12] Caliph (Khalīfah Rasūl Allah) essentially means successor to the messenger of God.

Roman rule, suffered greatly from a lack of stability, were without any passionate sense of loyalty, and were devoid of common purpose.

This disunity continued into the 7th century, which made them prime and relatively easy targets for subjugation by the Islamic armies. Most of the people they subjugated had only slight and fragile loyalties in the first place and cared little whether they paid taxes to their former leaders or to Islam.

On the other hand, the Eastern Roman Empire, sometimes called the Byzantine Empire, remained mostly intact following disintegration of the Western Roman Empire. Even though the Byzantine Empire remained intact, the inspired armies of Islam were able to quickly overrun Syria, which prompted the Byzantines to abandon their frontiers and withdraw into Anatolia (modern Turkey).

This move left Egypt relatively undefended and Egypt was soon subjugated to Islamic rule. This was the beginning of the centuries long effort by Islam to subdue the Byzantines. It was not until the fall of Constantinople, in 1453 that they finally succeeded.

In 644, Umar's reward for expanding Islam was his assassination by a Persian slave. And again, the prophet's son-in-law and nephew, Ali, for the third time, was not selected as Caliph, but was passed over for Uthman, although from the Quraysh tribe, he belonged to a different clan, the Umayyad.

Why Ali was thrice passed over seems to be unclear, since as he was from the same Hashemite clan as Muhammad and was the prophet's nephew and son-in-law, he seems to have been a natural choice. We can only assume that there were valid reasons for this passing-over, and his subsequent actions do provide clues.

Although Uthman would rule as Caliph for about 12 years, he added little to the territory of Islam and is best known for organizing and standardizing the Quran, which, at that time, was only allowed to be written in Arabic. During these early years, this rule had the effect of making Arabic the language of choice for both the religion and also for the administration, of the Islamic world.[13]

---

[13] As Islam spread, this rule was relaxed and today the Quran is available in many languages.

Apparently, Uthman was popular in the early part of his Caliphate, but when various protests began against him his popularity began to wane. The most dangerous of these protests was led, or at least instigated, by none other than Ali. Finally, in 656, the protests got out of hand and eventually Uthman was murdered.

Ali finally saw his chance, and immediately proclaimed himself Caliph. This action, accepted by some and rejected by many, quickly precipitated an internecine war that was to last until 661.

During this civil war, the first of several, Ali's grasp on the Caliphate was never firm, and, eventually, both he and his son, Hussein, were murdered. Following their deaths, they became the founding martyrs of the Shia branch of Islam, which today is dominant in Iran, prominent in Iraq, and exists in pockets throughout Islam.

To be Caliph was a powerful position, but since three of the first four were murdered, apparently, it was not a very secure position. Also, it should be mentioned, that it was this first civil war that saw the beginning of the blood feud between the Sunni and the Shia, which continues to this day.

Umayyad Dynasty (661 to 732)

The first civil war ended in 661 with the recognition of Muawiyah I, as Caliph. Muawiyah, like Uthman, was a member of the Umayyad clan of the Quraysh tribe. With the return of relative peace, Muawiyah was able, in his 19-year caliphate, to continue Islamic expansion, but his greatest contributions seem to have been an administrative reorganization of conquered territory that resulted in more efficient governing.

Following Muawiyah, there was a series of Umayyad Caliphs who were able to complete the expansion of Islam westerly through all of North Africa and into the Iberian Peninsula, while in the east the expansion was as far as Khurasan, which lies east of the Caspian Sea. It was also during this period that the second civil war occurred.

There is some confusion about the exact dates of the second civil war. Some say it started in 680 with the death of Muawiyah, while others say it started three years later with the death of his son, Yazid I, who had succeeded Muawiyah as Caliph. In any case, it was another one of those periods within the internal affairs of Islam where, because of the complex clan and tribal affiliations, it is difficult to follow the alliances and the hostilities.

In any case, the second civil war seems to have been concluded by 685, with the recognition of Abd Al-Malik as Caliph. He is best known as the Caliph who built several famous mosques, including the famous *Dome of the Rock* in Jerusalem. Building this mosque was significant since with the construction of this mosque and the one he built in Damascus, the center of Islam shifted permanently to the north away from Medina and Mecca, and into the Levant.

Although the Umayyad Dynasty lasted until 750, I have chosen to end this narrative in 732 for two reasons. First, this year marks the one hundredth anniversary of Muhammad's death, and, second, this was the year that Islam's expansion in western Europe was halted at the *Battle of Tours* in France. After that, Western Europe was never threatened again, but in Eastern Europe, Islam eventually came to occupy most of the Balkans and parts of Hungary.[14]

---

[14] The last great attempt to extend Islam into Europe was in 1683 with the Ottoman *Siege of Vienna*. With outside help from a Christian coalition, the siege failed and Islamic expansion in eastern Europe essentially ended and the Ottoman Empire began a long, slow period of decay that lasted until 1922.

As mentioned, the Umayyad Dynasty lasted until 750, when defeated in the *Battle of Zab* by a coalition of Abbasids, Shia, and Persians, and Abu Al-Abbas become the first Abbasid Caliph. The former Caliph, Marwan II, fled to Egypt, but was hunted down and killed, as were every male in his family, save one.

There were four Rashidun Caliphs, fourteen Umayyad Caliphs, but the Abbasid Caliphs lasted from 750 to 1517. Following the Abbasid Caliphates, there was a line of Caliphs that lasted until 1924, when the Ottoman Turks abolished the position and title of Caliph.

Final Comments

It is often asked how these Arabs, a backward people even by the standards of the time, were able to burst forth onto the world scene and, in a brief period, conquer such vast regions.

Part of the answer lies in their very poverty. Those with little to lose, saw great gains to be had for the taking, and take they did. It was a matter of the *have-nots* going after the *haves*. Most Arabs had never seen such lush lands, and compared to the vast Arabian desert, just about anywhere else seemed an improvement.

Additionally, Muhammad put forth a straight forward theology that was easy to understand, and unlike Christianity and Judaism, of the 7th century, was not cloaked in elaborate ritual and complex theology. Without doubt, his relatively simple message gave dignity and pride to the tribes of Arabia, who had always been in a backwater region such that even the Romans, seeing nothing of value, left them alone. They saw themselves as the *new* chosen people who were sanctioned to dominate.

These tribes of Arabia were in constant conflict with each other, and even the clans within a tribe had conflicts. This meant that to be a Bedouin male, was to be a fighter, which combined with their unbridled religious zeal, gave the Arab armies a fighting edge over most of their opponents. Plus, the new religion gave these tribes a unity that they had never experienced, and, through aggressive action, they were able to redirect their internal squabbles toward outsiders.

It has sometimes been said that as Islamic armies conquered new territories, the indigenous people were converted to Islam by force. This isn't altogether true. Because Muhammad believed that since Jews and Christians were also followers of Abraham, they could remain unconverted to Islam and unmolested.

Conquered Jews and Christians were allowed to practice their religions if they paid the taxes demanded by the Islamic governors. However, for all others, non-Abrahamic pagans, the message of the conquerors was simple; convert to Islam pay tribute - or die.[15]

---

[15] Quran: Chapter 9, Verse 5.

On the other hand, Muslims were not taxed, so there was always an incentive to convert and avoid taxation. In fact, so many voluntarily converted that tax revenues dropped dramatically, and it was finally declared that new converts would still be taxed, but at a lower rate.

Muhammad believed that the paths of Moses and Jesus were insufficient and would not last, and as the last great prophet, his message would last. He taught that those who fought for Islam would either gain temporal rewards, if they survived, or a celestial paradise if they didn't. A central tenet of his doctrine was the notion that he had God's permission to make war on non-believers.

Under Muhammed, Islam was an unfettered autocracy, and so it has remained up to today. This is most apparent in the kingdoms of Jordan (Hashemite) and Saudi Arabia (House of Saud), where the monarchs claim descent from the Prophet, and exercise considerable, if not absolute, power over their subjects.[16] These are the only two extant Islamic kingdoms, but there are other countries dominated by the Islamic religion that are essentially ruled by Islamic clerics under Islamic Law (Sharia). The best example is probably Iran, where the Ayatollah rules unquestionably.

---

[16] This seems especially true for Saudi Arabia where the House of Saud has, at least partially, adopted iconoclastic Wahhabism.

Coda

From what has been presented herein, it is obvious that these two religions had, from the beginning, as many differences as similarities. This is clearly shown by their very methods of expansion and conversion.

Being non-political was necessary for Christianity to co-exist in environments that if not overtly hostile, were also not overly friendly. On the other hand, Islam was necessarily political from the beginning. Christianity built up its following in urban enclaves scattered throughout the Roman Empire using persuasion, while Islam was spread territorially through forced subjugation.

Perhaps, the main difference was the manner in which each declared and executed their spiritual sanction. Islam claimed a sanction that justified violence to non-believers, while, in practice, there has always been and still is, almost constant internecine hostilities within Islam. This is in spite of the Quran, which specifically forbids internecine warfare between Muslims.[17]

Although, it seems that Muhammad entered Medina peacefully, his return to Mecca was the result of successful aggressive war against the citizens of Mecca. As stated previously, this set the pattern for all future expansion of Islam.

To be sure, Christianity had periods of internecine hostilities that occurred during the late medieval period and again starting with the Reformation. Soon after Luther posted his proclamation[18], hostilities started between the reformers and the Catholic Church. These overt hostilities lasted for more than a hundred years, until finally, and gradually, fading away by the end of the 17th century. However, even prior to the Reformation, there were episodes of descent, such as the Hussite Wars of the early 15th century.[19]

Early Christianity expanded without aggression toward non-believers, whether Jew or gentile, the choice to convert was always an individual choice, and not a choice dictated by political pressure. The early church

---

[17] Quran: Chapter 4, verses 92, 93.

[18] This is a reference to the *Ninety-Five Theses* that Luther published in 1517.

[19] See the essay herein: *The Thirty Years War*

had neither the means nor the inclination to coerce conversions. Even after Christianity was adopted by the Emperor Constantine, the government and military of the empire remained secular, with the church providing spiritual guidance.

It seems that Islam has remained closer to its original doctrines than has Christianity. However, on the other hand, Christianity can be said to have shed much of its medieval practices through the effect of the Reformation.

Although many of the ancient rituals are still maintained by the Catholic and Orthodox branches of Christianity, the Protestants have mostly abandoned the rituals of the past, with a few exceptions such as communion.

Of course, by the time of the Reformation, the Catholic and Orthodox traditions had accumulated almost 1500 years of doctrine and ritual that was, and still is, deeply embedded. On the other hand, the Reformation went much farther than the early advocates such as Martin Luther intended or considered necessary. Luther sought the reformation of Catholicism, not its replacement.

In any case, the Reformation resulted in changing Christian doctrine from scholarly works promulgated from within the established church hierarchy to a matter of opinion based on individual interpretation. This effort was much aided by the availability of Bible translations in the vernacular that were printed instead of copied by hand. After the Reformation, for many, Christianity, like Islam, practiced a much-simplified doctrine.

Finally, it should be noted that for hundreds of years, Islam and Christianity lived side by side in many of the regions annexed to Islam. For example, the Coptic Orthodox, in Egypt since the 1st century, has co-existed with Islam since the 7th century.

This co-existence existed through much, if not most, of the Middle East until the arrival and ascendency of the Seljuk Turks in the 11th century. These Seljuks swept in from the east and, after several successful battles, were able to annex a large territory that included most of the Levant and Anatolia.

In the late 11th century, it was claimed that after the Seljuk Turks took control of Jerusalem, Christian pilgrims were no longer protected and allowed unhindered access to this holy city. As news of the disruptions to pilgrimages spread throughout Europe, the stories became exaggerated, and eventually became the enflamed issues that directly led to the Crusades.

And, in turn, these Crusades, which occurred at intervals over a period of more than a hundred years, have been blamed for the tension that has existed between Islam and Christianity ever since. However, this is not altogether true, following the last Crusade to the Holy Land in the early 13th century, Christians again enjoyed free access to Jerusalem and other holy sites in the area.

Even later after the Seljuk's were displaced by the Ottomans, access to the Holy Land continue to be available, at first, since the Ottoman Empire was preoccupied with fighting against the Byzantines and the Persians in the East. The ottomans, not content in being the dominant power in western Asia after the fall of Constantinople (1453), used this solid foothold in Europe as a means of advancing deeper into the European continent.

And advance they did, through a series of decisive battles that were to become legends in themselves, they managed by the middle of the 16th century to advance through the Balkans, into Hungary just west of Buda, and into Wallachia, Transylvania, and Moldavia. Even today, the Balkan remain a region of strong religious ardor and as recently as the 1990's, one of these battles, the Battle of Kosovo (1389), was used as a motivation for open hostilities.

1.2 The Conquest of Mexico

*Reconsidering the Conquest and
How Cortes Won...*

Cast of Characters
[In order of mention]

Hernan Cortes: Spanish adventurer and leader of the Spanish Conquest of Mexico.

Montezuma II: Emperor of the Mexican Empire.

Diego Velázquez de Cuéllar: Spanish governor of Cuba.

Pedro de Alvarado: One of the Spanish Captains and second in command.

Pánfilo de Narváez: Commander of the punitive expedition sent to Mexico by the Cuban Governor.

1.2 The Conquest of Mexico

Introduction

Since the full story of the Conquest is long and complex, it is not the purpose here to recount the details of the conquest of Mexico, but rather to discuss how such a small band of Spaniards were able to subdue a large empire in the relatively short time of slightly more than two years.

Even when presented in the brief, as will be done here, it is a story of epic proportions that has few peers over the 4000-year history of epic stories that started with epic story of Gilgamesh and the stories of Homer.[20]

And like all true epics, this one is also a story of bravery, risk taking, and brutality, where these attributes are intermixed within the participants such that it is difficult to determine the good from the bad. There are no pure innocents and no pure villains. There are no true protagonists or antagonists, there are only humans playing their role in a drama where even the leaders often have little control over events.

It is the playing out of human drama set in the context of the early 16th century, where life and death were more out in the open than in the western world of today, and risk taking implied mortal risk.

This story is also an excellent example of the types of historical events that are easily transposed mentally and emotionally from the context of when they occurred, in this case the early 16th century, to a 21st century context.

Therefore, I have tried not to make any moral judgments of any of the participants, for that is not my purpose or intent. Judgment by 21st century context is a misrepresentation of the values of the time and if we have come to condemn certain practices of the past, however it should be remembered that 21st century mores are but a thin veneer that is easily stripped away.

However, it is sometimes necessary to comment on the social and religious conditions of the time, since it is only through understanding some of these conditions, can we understand how the Conquest turned out the way it did.

---

[20] The Gilgamesh epic is believed to date as far back as 2000BC, and Homer's stories about 800BC.

The Background

The Mexica[21]

By the year 1519, the Mexica were undisputed rulers of what today is central Mexico. Through conquest and intimidation, they had spent just over one hundred years building up a confederation of client states that were required to bring an exact tribute to the Mexican rulers residing in the capitol city of Tenochtitlan.

For example, this tribute required exact amounts of specific goods to be delivered every 80 days. The goods consisted of feathers, manufactured goods, various minerals, and, of course, gold and silver. This tribute brought wealth to the Mexica ruling class and economic stability to the citizens of this great city.

Although, constantly at war with one or another of their neighbors, the citizens of Tenochtitlan seemed secure in their island city.[22] Of their neighbors, only Tlaxcala to the east was still independent of the Mexica, and this independence was to play a major role in what occurred after the arrival of the Spanish.[23]

Tenochtitlan was actually part of a tri-city alliance, which included the neighboring cities of Texcoco and Tlacopan. Although an alliance, Tenochtitlan was the dominant partner and it was here that the Emperor Montezuma and his court resided. The Emperor had almost absolute religious and secular authority over the alliance, as well as the many districts and tribal areas throughout what is now central Mexico.

But all was not as secure as it might have seemed on the surface. For several years before the Spanish arrival, certain events and visions were noted that caused concern among the leadership. These events and visions were considered omens of ill fortune and are said to have caused the Mexica to

---

[21] I have adopted the convention Mexica that is used by Hugh Thomas (see bibliography) in his book on the Conquest. It is the name they called themselves and is pronounced Mesheeca. The name Aztec was not used by any of the participants in the Conquest. For example, Bernal Diaz, in his eye witness account, referred to them as Mexicans. The erroneous name Aztec was only made popular in the 18th century. I will use both Mexica and Mexican.

[22] Tenochtitlan was an island city in Lake Texcoco and was connected to the mainland by three causeways.

[23] Some have said that they left Tlaxcala un-subjugated because it served as a training ground for the young Mexican warriors.

1.2 The Conquest of Mexico

increase human sacrifice to a previously unheard-of level. Although the exact number of victims is unknown, according to witnesses, thousands were sacrificed in the years leading up to the arrival.[24]

It is well known that religions that practiced human sacrifice and cannibalism were also religions of pessimism and fear, where the security of the society relied on constant blood appeasement. If looked at from a modern point of view, it now seems apparent that the Mexican society, after being confronted by the Spanish, developed a fatalistic attitude toward the strange people who had boldly forced themselves into their lives.

The Spanish

On the other hand, the Spanish, of 1519, were at a peak of optimism and confidence. This optimism and confidence was directly related to two events that took place only a few years before, in 1492.[25]

The first of these was the subjugation of the Islamic province of Granada by the armies of newly united Castile and Aragon. Granada was the last Islamic possession within the Iberian Peninsula and its fall marked the end of a re-conquest of Iberia that had, literally, been going on for centuries.

The second event, in that same year, was the discovery of islands that became known as the West Indies. Both events reinforced Spanish confidence in their national identity and in their spiritual belief in the Catholic Church. Both events were seen as proof of God's favor toward the Spanish.

It seems that while the Spanish were gaining confidence, the Mexica were losing confidence. The collision between these two opposites was destined to be catastrophic.

---

[24] Recent excavations (2017) have apparently unearth remnants of the Templo Mayor Tzompantli (skull rack). It is believed that many thousands of skulls remain buried at that site.

[25] On 19 October 1469, Queen Isabella of Castile and King Ferdinand of Aragon were married and new kingdom of Castile and Aragon was formed.

The Conquest

In the interest of brevity, instead of going into details of the conquest, certain key episodes that essentially tell the story will be discussed.

When Hernan Cortes[26] started his voyage from Cuba, he was in open mutiny against the governor of Cuba, Diego Velázquez de Cuéllar. The governor had chartered the expedition as a trading mission and had placed Cortes in command, but when rumors began to circulate that, instead of just trading, Cortes intended to do more and establish a permanent colony on the coast of Mexico, the governor rescinded his charter and ordered that Cortes not be allowed to sail from Cuba. The rumors, of course, were true, and, on 18 February 1519, Cortes ignored this order and set sail.

The Arrival

After stops at the island of Cozumel and the coast of Yucatan, around June 3, Cortes and company finally landed on the coast of Mexico. Their early encounters with the natives, although initially friendly, quickly turned from friendly to hostile when the natives learned the Cortes had not come to trade, but to stay. This became apparent when Cortes had his company almost immediately start the construction of a town which he named Villa Rica de la Vera Cruz.[27] However, after some intermittent skirmishing, Cortes was able make a tentative peace.

It was also at this time, Cortes received his first gifts of gold from the ruler of the Mexica, Montezuma. These gifts were meant more as a bribe than a token of friendship, which Montezuma, wrongly, assumed would appease the strangers and they would leave, as the others who had come before had done.[28] However, this gesture, not surprisingly, only strengthened Cortes' resolve to advance cross country to the capitol.

It seems that not all of Cortes' men agreed with his mutiny and the change of plans from trade to colonization and wished to remain loyal to Velazquez. How many actually felt that way is unknown, but apparently,

---

[26] Cortes was born in Medellin, Spain, in the year 1485 to a family of the lesser nobility. It is interesting that he was also second cousin to Francisco Pizarro, who later became the conqueror of Peru.

[27] The 1519 town was somewhat north of the Veracruz of today.

[28] This is a reference to earlier expeditions that made contact along the Yucatan and Mexican coasts but were only exploring and trading voyages.

1.2 The Conquest of Mexico

they were enough for Cortes to feel threatened by the possibility of a counter-mutiny.

How Cortes solved this problem is an excellent example of calculated risk taking. He simply stripped his ships of all usable material and scuttled the remains. Although this seems a brazen and unwise act, it wasn't as foolish as it might seem. Prior to this, Cortes had sent one ship that was commanded by two of his closest associates, with most of the gold that had been collected up to that time, back to Spain as a gift (bribe) for the Carlos I, the Hapsburg king of Spain. Along with the gold, he also sent a lengthy letter seeking recognition and favor from the king.

Cortes was a man with considerable political savvy, and most likely realized that it was only a matter of time before Velasquez would sent a punitive expedition after him and his followers. This knowledge, plus the fact that he would need more gold if he was to buy his way out of his mutiny, is probably why he was anxious to move inland to the capitol city.

The Advance Inland

After several months spent building the town of Villa Rica, Cortes was finally ready, in early September, to advance inland. This advance to the interior, was against the wishes of Montezuma and there occurred several unsuccessful attempts to halt or, at least, hinder Cortes' advance. The most serious of these was Cortes' encounter with the Cholulans, which will be described below.

As Cortes advanced toward the interior of Mexico, he passed into the territory of the Tlaxcalans, where, after some fighting and some negotiations, he won the Tlaxcalans over as allies. This was mainly because, as mentioned above, they were in constant conflict with the Mexica and, apparently, because their leaders, who were impressed with Spanish fighting abilities, saw an opportunity in an alliance. As we shall see, this alliance with the Tlaxcalans was to prove faithful, as well as fateful, such that it was critical to the ultimate success of Cortes' expedition.

The Cholula Incident

On continuing from Tlaxcala, with the added assistance of hundreds of Tlaxcalan warriors and porters, Cortes came upon the town of Cholula, which was second in size only to Tenochtitlan and was a city known for its ceremonial pyramids, which included the largest known in the new world.[29] Here, at first, they were met with an outward expression of friendship and hospitality that put the Spaniards at ease.

However, this condition did not last long. It seems that Cortes was warned that the leadership of Cholula, acting on orders from Montezuma, were planning a surprise attack on the Spanish.

Being forewarned, Cortes, proactive as usual, decided to attack first. He did this by luring the nobility and city leaders of Cholula into the main temple area where his men promptly fell on the unarmed Cholulans and a massacre followed with, possibly, several thousand Cholulans being killed.

This act by the Spanish has been used by some modern historians as proof of the viciousness of Europeans against native people. However, it must be remembered that the Cholulans were about to do the same to the Spanish.

Did the Spanish fabricate the story of the plot against them to justify their actions, or was the plot true? We will never know for certain, but in other encounters, with various tribes along their route to Tenochtitlan, the Spanish did not engage in such acts and attempted to have peaceful relations with the natives whenever possible. In any case, by contemporary 16th century ethics, such a move by Cortes to pre-empt a move by a possible enemy would have been considered prudent and acceptable.

This incident at Cholula, although, by 21st century standards might be considered an act of terror, had the effect of establishing the Spanish with a reputation for ferocity that was to serve Cortes well as he continued his advance to Tenochtitlan. From then on, the many villages and towns encountered were mostly all too eager to accommodate the Spanish as they passed through, and Cortes was able to complete the journey to Tenochtitlan in relative peace.

The Arrival in Tenochtitlan

Finally, after a long and arduous journey and almost nine months after leaving Cuba, on November 8, 1519, Cortes arrived at Tenochtitlan. Cortes and the company, which now include about 2000 Tlaxcalans, were welcomed as friendly visitors, and, after a formal welcome from the Emperor himself, the Spanish and their allies were lavishly housed in several of the many palaces within the city and well treated.

---

[29] The Great Pyramid of Cholula is 180 feet tall, and its base measures 1300 by 1300 feet.

1.2 The Conquest of Mexico

Unfortunately, following this initial welcome, this period of peace lasted only about a week. Somehow, Cortes learned that several of his men who had been left behind in Villa Rica had been murdered, supposedly by order of Montezuma.

In response to this act, Cortes' reacted decisively and had Montezuma taken prisoner as a hostage. What is surprising, is that this kidnapping was, apparently, accomplished without much difficulty, and without any real resistance from the people of Tenochtitlan. Perhaps, this was because Montezuma and the Mexica leadership were still uncertain about who these strangers really were.

It is also possible that this lack of resistance was an indication of defeatism and a sense of inevitability that prevailed within Mexican society. Apparently, the Mexican religion included a strong sense of predestination, which would include a belief in inevitability and lack of life choices.

In any case, this taking of Montezuma as hostage was another example of Cortes' boldness and, perhaps, impulsive use of calculated risks. However, as we shall see, Cortes' boldness and skills as a leader would again be demonstrated later with arrival of the punitive expedition, sent by the Governor of Cuba. But that was in the future, and for months, after the kidnapping, nothing much happened.

The Spaniards and even their Tlaxcalan allies were treated well, and with time on their hands, the Spaniards busied themselves with sending scouting parties into neighboring tribal areas in search of the sources of gold and silver. It was the calm before the storm.

Finally, after more than five months in Tenochtitlan, this period of peace came to an end, in April 1520, when Montezuma informed Cortes that a large number of ships had appeared at Villa Rica. Cortes, of course, knew immediately that this would be the anticipated punitive expedition sent by Governor Velázquez. However, he told Montezuma, probably with an air of bravado, that these ships were his reinforcements and re-supply.

The Narvaez Incident
The new arrivals had indeed been sent by Velasquez and were under the command of Pánfilo de Narvaez with 19 ships and about 1300 men, while

Cortes had with him less than 200 men.[30] Clearly, the odds did not favor Cortes.

Because, at that time, only about half of his company was in Tenochtitlan, Cortes was only able to take about 80 men with him to the coast to confront the new arrivals. This left about 120 men under the command of Cortes' second in command, Captain Pedro de Alvarado, to guard Montezuma and maintain peace in Tenochtitlan.

The story of how Cortes was able to meet and overcome this threat is beyond the scope of this work, but it can be said that he used his usual combination of surprise attack, diplomacy, bribery, and charm to defeat this expedition and incorporate most of Narvaez's troops into his company. Apparently, they preferred the prospect of gold over their punitive mission.

Having been successful in turning this threat to his advantage, Cortes soon started his return to Tenochtitlan with the addition of more than 1000 men, 96 horses, and other much needed equipment. However, the real storm was yet to arrive.

The Night of Sorrows

On or about June 24, 1920, after an absence of about two months, Cortes and company arrived back in Tenochtitlan, and to his great dismay, he finds that the people of Tenochtitlan are in revolt against the Spanish.

He also finds that the reason for this was the callous and unwise act by his captain, Pedro de Alvarado, who, for reasons that are not clear, attacked a large group of unarmed nobles, who had gathered for a religious festival, and murdered hundreds of them.[31]

Needless to say, Cortes was not too happy with Alvarado, but there was no time for recriminations when both the Spanish and their allies were fighting for survival. The city populous had risen up against the Spanish, and the entire company had been forced by overwhelming numbers to retreat into their lodgings and fight defensively for their lives.

---

[30] There were already about 100 men loyal to Cortes at the coast.

[31] Alvarado was later to demonstrate a savagery against the native populations that has given all conquistadors a bad name. To be sure, none were saints, but many were just looking for a better life.

1.2 The Conquest of Mexico

If that wasn't bad enough, just a few days later, on June 29, Montezuma, who was pleading with his citizens to cease fighting, was struck by a rock and mortally wounded. His sudden death, whether by accident or design, was blamed on the foreigners such that the Mexica became even more determined to destroy the Spanish and their attacks increased in ferocity.[32] Cortes knew that he was in a desperate situation, and quickly decided that their only chance of survival was to breakout of the city.

The very next day, on the night of June 30th, Cortes and the assembled company attempted to break out of the city. All the Spanish and their allies, mostly Tlaxcalans, moved suddenly to force their way across the western causeway, which was the shortest route out of the city to the mainland. This attempt was almost immediately noticed, and as the alarm spread throughout the city, thousands of warriors and citizens swarmed out to fight the Spanish.

What followed was almost a complete ruin of the expedition. As they tried to fight their way across the causeway, they were slaughtered by the hundreds. Although Cortes and some of his company were able to pull off their escape, more than 800 of the soldiers were either killed outright or captured for later sacrifice.[33]

This *Night of Sorrows*, as it came to be known came close to total destruction of the Spanish and ending any chance Cortes had of success. However, Cortes, always the strong leader, managed to rally his surviving soldiers and allies to stage a fighting retreat to Tlaxcala where they found refuge and began to recover from their wounds.

Given the condition of the Spanish after fleeing Tenochtitlan, they were fortunate that the pursuit by the Mexicans was not as determined as it could have been. For the most part, the Mexicans simply harassed the fleeing company who were only forced to fight a single formal battle, which the Spanish won after killing several of the enemy leaders. Perhaps, the Mexican leaders thought that the Spanish were vanquished and would leave them in peace.

---

[32] Some claim that the Spanish killed Montezuma, but this would not have been to their advantage. Most likely he was accidentally killed in the confusion of the fighting.

[33] It is said that many of the soldiers, especially the new ones, burdened themselves with as much gold and silver that they could carry, and because of this extra weight, they drowned in the lake.

Although rid of the Spanish, within weeks after the they were gone, smallpox developed within the island city and many thousands began to die.[34] This, of course, weakened the Mexicans ability to defend their city and was a major factor in what followed. Although, the epidemic was unintended, the Spanish were again fortunate, since the population of Tenochtitlan was greatly reduced and weakened.

The Recovery and Preparation
Aided by the lack luster pursuit by the Mexica, the surviving company was able to struggle back to Tlaxcala, and here the Spanish remained in Tlaxcala for several months. This was necessary because according to the eye witness, Bernal Diaz, everyone including Cortes had at least one wound, and many had multiple wounds.

While recuperating in Tlaxcala, several merchant ships arrived at Villa Rica with much needed supplies, which were immediately purchased by Cortes.[35] Additionally, to improve his supply situation, he. Prudently avoided Cuba, by sending two of Narvaez' ships to Hispaniola to buy supplies. Also, during this time, additional reinforcements arrived such that Cortes was able to build up an army of more than a thousand soldiers.

Finally, on December 28, 1520, after almost six months of recovery and preparation, Cortes was ready to leave Tlaxcala and begin to execute his plans for retaking Tenochtitlan.

The Fall of Tenochtitlan
During the period of recovery and preparation, Cortes had implemented what today might be called a secret weapon. This was the construction of thirteen boats that would be used to counter the many canoes that the Mexica used so effectively to attack the Spaniards during the Night of Sorrows. These boats, besides removing the menace of the native canoes, would also be used to provide flank protection for the soldiers fighting their way across the three causeways that led to the island city.

Each boat had both sails and oars, a small brass cannon, and a crew of 25 men which included both those assigned to handle the boat and other men

---

[34] It is strange that this happened after the Spanish were forced from the city, since following the defeat, the Mexica sacrificed about 70 Spanish prisoners. It is possible, that contact with the body fluids of the victims this caused the epidemic?

[35] By this time, the Cortes expedition was well known throughout the Indies.

1.2 The Conquest of Mexico

to fight. Twelve of the boats were forty feet in length and one was about forty-eight feet long and was reserved as flagship for Cortes. Some authors have called these boats brigantines, some have called them sloops, and they have even been called launches, in any case, they provided the extra mobility and fighting edge that Cortes needed.

The construction of these boats is another example of the resourcefulness and energy of the Spanish. Their construction was a major accomplishment that required considerable skill and a type of determination that the Mexica lacked.

Finally, on May 22, 1521, almost a year after the Night of Sorrows, all was finally ready, and the siege of Tenochtitlan began. Cortes understood the value of first controlling the lake and started his siege with a series of water fights where these boats easily over whelmed the lightweight Mexican canoes.

After obtaining control of the lake, Cortes then started attacks on all three of the causeways. He also managed to cut the aqueduct that brought fresh water to the city, which along with control of the lake, he was able to severely limit the re-supply of food and fresh water to the city inhabitants.

But even in a weakened state, the Mexica fought hard and progress in the fighting on the causeways was measured in feet gained per day. This way, the siege lasted almost 3 months, until, on August 13, when the new emperor of Mexico, Cuauhtémoc, was capture, the fighting was finally over. With the capture of the Emperor, again the city was leaderless, and the will to fight quickly evaporated and on the very day of the emperor's capture the Spanish were able to occupy the city.

Recapitulation: How Cortes Won

As mentioned in the *Introduction*, the two cultures of Mexico and Spain, once they met, were destined, by their similarities and differences to be in conflict.

In similarities, the Mexica were, like the Spanish, arrogant and aggressive toward their respective neighbors. The Mexica were constantly at war with one or more of the local tribes, and, the same can be said about the Spanish, who after the defeat of the Moors of Granada, were free to join in the warfare going on, at that time, in Italy.

Both cultures were very class minded such that persons lived and died much as their parents and grandparents had. In both cultures, rising above one's birth-class was usually only possible through religious office or through exemplary military service.

However, it is in their differences that we find the characteristics of both cultures that inevitably led to open conflict between these two cultures. The greatest differences, and the most obvious point of conflict, can be found in the differences between their respective religions.

Within both cultures, their religions were the final authority that, at least in theory, superseded secular rule. For example, the emperor of Mexico was trained for the priesthood prior to being emperor, and the King of Spain was anointed by the Pope in Rome,[36] which implied a superior position. But there was the difference that the Emperor of Mexico was effectively the head priest, while the King of Spain only had secular authority and deferred matters of religion to the clergy.

Catholicism, as practiced by the Spanish, was optimistic, dogmatic, and uncompromising in its belief in the righteousness of their actions. Just as their aggressive actions against the followers of Islam or their fellow Christians were felt justified; by extension, their actions against the native population of the Indies were also justified. The subjugation of the indigenous population of the Indies was seen as missionary work. When the Spanish arrived somewhere, they carried a cross in one hand, and a sword in the other.

Dis-similarly, the religion of the Mexica was a religion of constant fear, perpetuated by the incessant need to appease their gods through pious

---

[36] Carlos I, was king of Spain and also the Holy Roman Emperor as Charles V.

1.2 The Conquest of Mexico

ceremonies augmented with human sacrifice and cannibalism. They believed that it was only through these sacrifices that they could retain favor from the gods. They also believed in a type of pre-destination that predicted the end of the world in the near future.

In summary, a partial listing of attributes that the Spanish possessed includes a positive religion, optimism, arrogance, an aggressive spirit, and iron technology, while the Mexica possessed a negative religion, pessimism, arrogance, a defeatist spirit, and pre-bronze-age technology.

In the years preceding the Spanish arrival, the Mexica had experienced a series of omens that were interpreted as proof of their immanent end. Not the least of these was the first sightings off their coast of floating islands inhabited by strange man-like creatures with long beards. These *creatures* were, of course, the Spanish and the *floating islands* were their ships.

Another major difference was their relative level of technology. Although, complex socially and accomplished artistically,[37] the Mexica were pre-bronze age with regard to metal technology. The only metals they worked were gold, silver, and copper. They also lacked any beasts of burden, which meant that travel and movement of goods was done on foot.

However, when discussing technology, we must be careful and not confuse the level of technology with the level of social sophistication and complexity. The technical and the social exist more or less independently but are often wrongly equated such that one is considered causally connected to the other.

Superior technology does not necessarily mean social superiority. For example, when it came to warfare, the technology of the Spanish weaponry was far superior to the obsidian edged weapons of the Mexica, but a bigger difference was in their chosen methods of warfare.

When the Mexica fought, their goal was more to obtain captives, rather than destroy their enemies fighting capability or will to fight. The highest honors that a Mexican warrior could receive was through capture of enemies for sacrifice. In fighting between the tribes, fatal casualties were

---

[37] When viewing the works of art that Cortes had sent to the King of Spain. The famous painter, Albrecht Durer, was said to have greatly marveled at the quality of the works. Of course, Durer wasn't the only one, all who saw these artifacts expressed similar reactions. Carlos I traveled extensively, even to England, and to impress his subjects and allies, he took many of these artifacts along.

never too great, and the goals mostly limited to obtaining captives or as a disciplinary act of force against client tribes.

On the other hand, the Spanish fought with the goal of destroying the capability and/or will of their foes to continue fighting, which was aided, unintentionally, by the Mexican's goal of obtaining captives. According to the eye witness, Bernal Diaz, the Mexica would try to incapacitate and capture their foes, while avoiding any fatal wounds.

The result was that the Spanish, although wounded many times during the conquest, had improved chances of survival. Bernal claims that he participated in more than a hundred skirmishes and battles. This is probably not an exaggeration since the siege of Tenochtitlan lasted 75 days and came at the end of two years of intermittent fighting, which had offered many opportunities for close-in fighting.

Although the steel weapons of the Spanish were superior to those of the Mexica, the wooden, obsidian embedded swords of the Mexica were much respected by the Spanish. Although the obsidian was brittle, it was also very sharp and could easily inflict serious cuts or even sever a limb.[38]

However, initially, it was the horse that gave the Spanish a tactical edge. The indigenous population was, at first, terrified of the horsemen and for a short time even thought man and horse were a single creature. This was soon disproved, and fear of the horse was lessened after one of them was killed in a skirmish. But, even after that, the power of charging horsemen was hard to resist.

Even given technical superiority, the Spanish and their allies were still greatly outnumbered. History has many examples where a small, but determined and inspired band, was able to hold out against all but impossible odds, but in essentially all of these cases, the small band was eventually overwhelmed. This did not happen to the Spanish.

These small bands were almost exclusively on the defensive against superior forces, which, generally speaking, gave them a temporary advantage, but the opposite is true of the Spanish. The Spanish went on the offensive against their foe, and it was the Mexica who made the mistake of shutting themselves up defensively in Tenochtitlan, where they remained waiting for the Spanish.

---

[38] Besides the usual cutting weapons, the Spanish also had crossbows, arquebuses (muskets), and several small cannons.

1.2 The Conquest of Mexico

Unfortunately, without accurate records, the exact number of Spanish soldiers and their allies are impossible to determine. After being reinforced in the months following the retreat from Tenochtitlan, a reasonable estimate is that, at the closing stage of the conquest, the Spanish had somewhere between 1200 and 1500 soldiers and their allies, mostly Tlaxcalans, numbered between 10,000 and 15,000.[39]

On the other hand, the Mexica, even after having the population decreased by smallpox, would still have been able to field 40,000 to 50,000 warriors. These odds seemed to favor the Mexica, but mere numbers were not the only factor.

It is a mystery why, after forcing the Spanish out of Tenochtitlan, the Mexicans did not make an all-out attempt to finish off the Spanish. At that time, the Spanish and their surviving allies were exhausted, and most were wounded during the flight from the city, but, even with this disadvantage, the pursuit by the Mexicans resulted in only a single fixed battle (Battle of Otumba) that was won by the Spanish, after they managed to kill several Mexican leaders. After which, in typical fashion, the rest of the Mexica simply drifted away.

Surely, this weak pursuit, among other things, indicates a lack of morale and resolve. Whether they thought that the Spanish would leave them in peace or they were content to sacrifice the many captives from the Night of Sorrow, is not known.

Believing in pre-destination, it is also possible that they were simply resolved to await their fate, as if they had no other choice. We will never know the exact mental state of the Mexica, but we do know that when the Spanish came back to lay siege to Tenochtitlan, they were highly motivated and had the tactical advantage.

As mentioned before, the building of the small fleet of brigantines, was equivalent to what today we would call a *secret weapon*. Once launched, these boats, each with 25 men, a small cannon, crossbowmen, and musketeers, and either through firepower or by simply ramming the fragile canoes were able to quickly gain the ascendency over the hundreds of native canoes that had previously dominated Lake Texcoco.

---

[39] Some have estimated that the Spanish allies numbered up to 40,000 or more. This is likely an exaggeration.

The second tactical advantage was a result of the geography of Tenochtitlan. The protection nominally provided by being an island city with access through only three causeways now worked against them.

When the Mexica had command of the lake, as they did on the Night of Sorrows, they could out flank any enemies attempting to cross the causeways into the city and cause them great harm. However, by shutting themselves in the city, and with the command of the lake now in the hands of the Spanish, their superior numbers were less effective.

This is because, these causeways, broken by several bridged gaps, were so narrow that only a few warriors at a time could be effective against the Spanish. With the boats providing flank support, the Spanish were able to attack along all three causeways. Using this combination, of land and water forces, the Spanish and their allies made slow, but continuous progress in their advanced towards the city proper.

With the Mexicans exposed in front and on both side by Spanish firepower, inevitably, the Spanish were able to push their way across the causeways and into the outskirts of the city. Still, even with the water and food supplies all but cut off, they put up a determined fight and the Spanish could only measure progress slowly.

Finally, on August 13, 1521, after almost three months of siege, the new emperor, Cuauhtémoc, was captured trying to flee the city in a canoe. That very day, the fight came to a halt, and the Spanish and their allies took possession of the city as masters of the Valley of Mexico.

Becoming leaderless again, they were no longer capable of organized resistance. This phenomenon had been witnessed by the Spanish before in prior battles. Once deprived of one or more of their leaders, the fighting would soon stop, and the warriors would drift away.

In a real sense, the difference between success and failure was imbedded in the cultures of the antagonists. The fatalism of the Mexica proved to be their undoing, while the tenacity and purposefulness of the Spanish led them to victory.

1.2 The Conquest of Mexico

Appendix: Conquest versus Colonizing

Starting in the late 15th century, what is now called the Americas (South, Central, and North) began coming under the influence and eventual domination of people from western Europe.

Starting in central and south America, the colonization of undeveloped territory accelerated throughout the 16th century while the indigenous population, primitive in technology, but in most cases, well developed socially, was either intentionally displaced or inadvertently reduced through deceases that they had previously not experienced, and for which they had no immunity.

Coincidentally, the northern part (now the US and Canada) was mostly occupied by northwestern Europeans, principally English and French, while the central and southern regions were mainly occupied by southwestern Europeans, principally Spanish with the major exception of the Portuguese in Brazil.

It was the cultural differences and differences in motivations between Europeans of the north and those of the south that resulted in two very distinct styles of interaction with the indigenous populations. But of at least equal importance, the indigenous societies of the north and south differed greatly in social structure and world views.

The tribes of North America were socially well organized and practiced a form of animistic religion that in some cases was of the *anima mundi* variety, while in the Mesoamerica there was a form of Animism that included human sacrifice. These differences played an important role in how they interacted with the strangers from Europe, and how each region was assimilated differently by the Europeans.

In the early English colonies, there was very little social interaction between natives and colonists. Their relations were mostly formal in the sense of maintaining very separate life styles and almost complete segregation. On the other hand, the French in North America, who came to trade and not to colonize in the English sense, had a much closer relationship with the native population. However, it was the Spanish who interacted the most with the natives.

They, like the early French, did not come with families and consequently intermingled with the locals to a much higher degree than even the French. This seems to have been especially true from the time of the Conquest of

Mexico forward. Cortes, himself, and many, if not most, of his troops had close relations with the women of Mexico. Native women were routinely *converted* to Christianity, given Cristian names, and married off to a Spaniard.

Reasons for this difference are many, but one of the primary seems to be inherent in the different methods and motivations. The English, and the French, although to a lesser degree, colonized for a new place to live where they thought they would be unfettered by many of the traditional social aspects of Europe.

It is well known that many early English settlers were seeking to escape religious persecution that was active in early 17th century England. A look at the early history of the English colonies in North America shows that several of the colonies were established simply as a political entity that would protect their particular religious beliefs.

On the other hand, Spanish colonization was motivated by the desire to obtain wealth and status. Consequently, most Spanish invaders were men looking for easy wealth and family units were rare.

Beyond the differences in motivation for colonizing, the early English colonies were, for the most part, founded and inhabited by fundamental Protestants who considered themselves above the natives in both a cultural and racial sense. On the other hand, the Spanish and French did not have the same racial and social biases toward the native population.

This separation of the native people within English colonies has continued into the present where the reservation system insures that this separation will continue. Currently there are 562 native tribal affiliations that are formally recognized by the US government. Not all tribes have a reservation, but those tribes that do, have allocated parcels of land that vary in size from a less than two acres to more than 17 million acres!

Obviously, these allocations have an element of arbitrariness and likely reflect something about the quality of the land as well as the ability of the tribe to negotiate more favorable treatment. It is not surprising that the largest reservations are in the western part of the US and occupy land that the US government of the 19th century thought less desirable or even worthless.

The bottom line is that in the US, the Amerindians who reside on reservations remain, for the most part, isolated from mainstream society. Because of various political and social agendas, this reservation system, which fosters a mentality of entitlement and essentially assures poor living conditions will, to the detriment of many, likely continue well into the future.

In recent years, the phenomenon of so-called *Indian Gaming* has brought living standard improvements for only a small minority of Amerindians, while the great majority remain impoverished. Indian Gaming was *sold* to the American public as a means of establishing self-reliance for the reservation Indians. For example, televised ads played up an emotional plea to help the Indians out of poverty, and the public bought into this scheme.

What actually happened was that a small minority of the tribal members have benefited from these casinos, while the majority of tribal members still live in poverty. This is due, in part, because a significant percentage of the profits go to outside corporations that own major stakes in these casinos. The truth is that these Amerindian casinos are only extensions of the Las Vegas and Atlantic City gambling interests.

In any case, the whole idea of nations within a nation was a short-sighted decision, and those who made these short-sighted decisions could not see how this would create an obstacle and ensure continued poverty and isolation. Given the overall political attitude that exists within the US today, the anachronism of the reservation system is likely, to the detriment of all, continue indefinitely.

1.3 The First Thirty Years War: 1618-1648

Reconsidering Motives and Consequences...

Introduction

By the middle of the 15th century, Italy was well into the high Renaissance, England was in the middle of a civil war, France was finally able to firmly incorporate former English possessions into the Kingdom of France, and central Europe was still a loose amalgam of more than 200, mostly, German speaking principalities.

Of the many notable events that took place in Europe at about that time, the two most significant were the sack of Constantinople (1453) by the Ottoman Empire and the election of Alfons de Borja (Borgia) as Pope Callixtus III (1455-1458).

The fall of Constantinople and the demise of the ancient Byzantine Empire, brought aggressive Islam into eastern Europe to stay such that the repercussions of this are still with us today.

The second event introduced into Italy a half century of Borgia hedonism, rampant nepotism, and, an attempt through aggressive warfare, assassination, and convenient marriages to create a new kingdom in Italy.

Nepotism and other forms of corruption reached new heights under the short reign of this first Borgia Pope, which was only exceeded by his nephew, Rodrigo de Borgia, who as Pope Alexander VI (1492-1503), along with Alexander's son, Cesare Borgia (1475-1597).

Although, stories about Alexander's and Cesare's behaviors were often exaggerated, the truth was enough such that it must be considered a major source of discontent and scandal within Italy that soon spread throughout the European community. Central and northern part of Europe was far enough removed from Rome such that what Papal influence did reach this

1.3 The First Thirty Years War: 1618-1648

far was diluted to the point of being mostly either ineffective or simply ignored.

In any case, this rampant corruption and disruption of the peace were enough such that by 1500 there was already a well-established anti-papal movement in central Europe that extended even into Scandinavia, and it was this movement that provided considerable fuel to the fire of discontent, which led to the Reformation.

It could be said that the origins of this war are to be found a hundred years earlier in the Reformation of the 16th century, but perhaps the roots go even deeper and we should search back to the 15th century (and earlier). Here, in addition to the Papal scandals and general mis-conduct mentioned above, we find the Hussite Wars that disrupted the peace central and eastern Europe for most of that century.

Of course, we could go back two more centuries to the Albigensian (1209-1229), the Bosnian (1235-1241), or the Aragonese (1284-1285) *crusades* that also pitted Christian against Christian.

These internecine Christian wars are usually, on the Catholic side, referred to as crusades, and like all such religious wars, these wars were exceptionally brutal with neither side sparing the other from hateful atrocities.

These revolts against the established church, came at the end of the medieval period in Europe, and at the beginning of the Renaissance in southern Europe, especially Italy. Besides the flourishing of the humanities, that is most associate with the Renaissance, this was also a period when strong national identities were forming, and national boundaries were being established.

There are many historical threads that could be followed, which occasionally intertwine and eventually lead us to the 17th century and the First Thirty Years War, but that would be too much of a divergence from the story to be told here.

It is sufficient to understand that unlike the usual internecine dynastic and territorial wars that had been the rule for over a thousand years, this war of Christian against Christian started as a conflict between their religious beliefs and the right of self-determination. That is, the hostilities were based on confessional differences of opinion within the various branches of Christianity that formed throughout the 16th century.[40]

Early in the Reformation, what started out as discussion and debate about abuses and corruption within the Church, quickly turned to an open challenge of the Papal authority in Rome. On the other hand, after enjoying supremacy for over a thousand years, and in order to maintain this supremacy, the Pope was more than willing to aggressively suppress any heretical or apostate movements.

The fact of the matter is that both sides seem to have been all too eager in moving to open hostilities, and within a few years after the start of the Reformation, in 1517, open warfare began. The first sizable conflict was the German Peasant Revolt of 1524, which was followed by periods of relative peace alternating with periods of open war the was to last for more than a century.

In 1555, almost forty years after Luther's famous posting, 224 German political entities were able to agree to a treaty known as the *Peace of Augsburg*. Within the terms of this treaty, the German states were free to choose either the Catholic or the Lutheran confessional.

That is, the rulers of these entities could choose one or the other, and their subjects were required to conform, or leave. This helped the German states to settle down a little, but in other countries, such as France and England, there was continued conflict.

Although this agreement was somewhat helpful in reducing tensions, by the early 1600's, matters were complicated by the revolt within the Spanish possessions in northern Europe called the Spanish Netherlands. In this revolt the Dutch had a two-fold incentive. The first, was the occupation by Spanish soldiers, and the second, was the differences between the Catholic Spanish and the Protestant Dutch.

The geographic separation of Spain and the Netherlands, meant the Spain had a vested interest in what was happening in certain western German states. This was partly due to the fact that other than by sea, the only other way that the Spanish could communicate with their northern possessions

---

[40]Part of the discontent within the Christian communities was the translations of the Bible from Latin and Greek into the vernacular that made many to begin questioning the primacy of the Roman Church. This questioning was due as much to what wasn't in the Bible as what was in the Bible.

was by passing through several German states. Not surprisingly, this passage often led to friction between Spain and these German states.

However, although the revolt in the Netherlands was important, it was the confessional and political differences throughout central Europe that led ultimately to open warfare.

Major Phases of the War

Given the length of the war and complexity of the various national and religious interests, and in the interest of brevity, only a few highlights of this conflict will be discussed.

Fortunately, it is fairly easy to break up the war into several periods or phases, which will give a general idea of the flow and provide some understanding of the complexity of this war that was, by far, the largest in terms of size of the armies involved, geographic spread, and amount of destruction that Europe had seen, up to that time.

Even today after about 400 years, the scope and impact of the Thirty Years War has only been exceeded by the world wars of the 20th century.

Bohemian Conflict (1618-1625)

In May of 1618, tensions between the German Emperor[41], Ferdinand I, and the protestants of Bohemia had almost reach the breaking point, when several Catholic envoys from the Emperor arrived in Prague to meet with certain Protestant leaders.

This famous meeting was held on the 3rd floor of the Bohemian Chancellery, and after some discussion and many accusations, three of Catholic envoys were grabbed and thrown out of a window, which was about 70 feet above the ground.

Somehow, all three managed to survive the fall, but after this incident, the time for negotiations was over and both sides prepared for open warfare. The *Defenestration of Prague*, as this incident became known, marked the beginning of the first phase of the war that was to last thirty years.[42]

Had this revolt remain a local affair, it might have been concluded in a relatively short time, but the Protestants of Bohemia needed allies, so they petitioned the German Protestant League for membership, which would

---

[41] The Holy Roman Emperor was sometimes called the German Emperor. This title started in the year 800 with the coronation of Charlemagne and ended in 1806 with the abdication of Francis II.

[42] This was actually the second defenestration of Prague, the first had occurred in 1419 during the Hussite wars when seven members of the Prague city council were thrown out of a window of the city hall. In this case, unlike the second, none survived.

1.3 The First Thirty Years War: 1618-1648

provide them with both financial and military support. On the other side, the new Emperor Ferdinand I also needed support, so he turned to the Spanish for aid.

These actions and others soon transformed a local affair into one that would eventually involve most of Europe, including the Scandinavian countries. But that was in the future, and the fate of this revolt was soon settled on November the 8th, 1620.

This settlement was the decisive victory of the Catholic League over the Protestants at the *Battle of White Mountain*, which took place near Prague.[43] After the defeat, the Bohemian Protestant cause was lost, and the nobility of Bohemia were able to reestablish Catholicism and switch Bohemia over to the Catholic League.

After the decisive Battle of White Mountain, the war between 1620 to 1625 took place in different parts of Europe and the hostilities were mostly small actions that were more like diversions. This is partly because during this period, several of the larger countries had internal problems that required attention.

For example, Poland was occupied with conflict against the Ottomans, France was occupied with fighting the Huguenots, the Spanish were occupied in the Palatinate and the Netherlands, and the English had their own internal problems that soon led to civil war. Because of all these diversions and the need to refit and rebuild the armies, it was more a period of consolidation and maneuver where the fighting was mostly minor skirmishing and sieges.

Danish Intervention (1625-1629)

This period of scattered conflict came to an end when, partly in support of the Protestant cause and partly because they felt threatened by the successes of the Catholic League, the Danes, under King Christian IV, decided to enter the war.

Although, the Danish intervention started with great aspirations, within the first year the Danes lost two battles, and after that they were essentially

---

[43] As an indication of the size of this wat, the combined armies at White Mountain totaled over 40,000. A very large number for those day, but also a number that would grow as the war progressed. For example, at the First Battle of Breitenfeld (1631) the total strength of the armies was more than 70,000.

on the defensive as the Catholic League pushed into Mecklenburg, Pomerania, and into Denmark (Jutland Peninsula). Here the League was stopped short of Copenhagen, only because they had no fleet with which to invade the island city.

However, the Danes were not defeated, Christian, after a pause for rebuilding his army, was again ready to take on the Catholic League. Once again, in 1628, Christian suffered yet another defeat.

After no successes in three years, apparently the Danes had had enough, and soon negotiations began that led, in 1629, to the *Treaty of Lubeck*. This treaty left Christian IV in a fairly good position, but the treaty effectively took the Danes out of the war.

Swedish Intervention (1630-1635)
With the arrival of a Swedish army under the Swedish King, Gustavus Adolphus, the year 1630 saw the arrival on the scene of another protestant threat to the Catholic League.

Expecting that the Swedes would suffer the same fate as the Danes, the initial success of the Swedes was a big surprise. In the first two years, they won two of the most significant battles of the war – the *Battle of Breitenfeld* (1631) and the *Battle of Lutzen (1632)*. Unfortunately, the Swedish King was killed at the second battle.

Following these two destructive battles, both sides needed to rest and regroup, so not much happened until 1634, when the Swedes, without their king, were soundly beaten at the *First Battle of Nordlingen*.

Again, as was usually the case after a major battle, both sides needed time to recover such that by the spring of 1635, and after the usual extended negotiations, the Imperial Catholics and Protestants were able to come to an agreement. This agreement was the treaty known as the *Peace of Prague*, which, among other things, effectively divided, with some expectations, the German states into Catholic in the south and Lutheran Protestants in the north[44].

---

[44] Only Catholics and Lutheran Protestants were included in this agreement, other Protestant sects, such as the Calvinists, were excluded. That is, this treaty essentially reinstated the *Peace of Augsburg* treaty of 1555.

1.3 The First Thirty Years War: 1618-1648

French Intervention (1635-1648)

By 1635, Cardinal Richelieu, Louis XIII's chief minister, was concerned about the ability of the Swedes to continue their participation in the war and having effectively solved the Huguenot problem, France was free to act. Additionally, France was unhappy with the terms of the *Peace of Prague* agreement, decided it was time to intervene. Since France was, and is, a Catholic country, it might be expected that they would side with the Imperial forces.

However, they joined forces with the Protestant Swedes instead. This is just one indication that, by the mid-point of the war, national interests were gaining precedence over confessional differences.

Consequently, France declared war on Spain in May of 1635 and then on the Holy League in August of 1636. However, for all its military might, France's efforts were a disaster. Spain was able to invade French soil and ravaged several French provinces. The Spanish even managed to threatened Paris, but the city was saved by a Spanish defeat in the *Battle of Breisach* in 1638. This battle turned the tide for France and by 1640, the Spanish had been forced to withdraw from French soil.

French ascendency in the war continued with a series of victories, including the *Siege of Arras (1640)*, which was made famous by its inclusion in Edmond Rostand's play, *Cyrano de Bergerac*.

This successful siege was followed by another French victory in 1643 at the *Battle of Rocroi*. Additional French victories followed, but neither side was willing to give up, and, although the Thirty Years War was concluded in 1648, the private conflict between Spain and France continued until 1659.

Peace of Westphalia (1648)

Finally, after four years of negotiations, peace finally came to Europe, or, at least, the Thirty Years War came to an end with the Peace of Westphalia. This treaty is generally considered the end of the war, but actually, it was a series of treaties that ended in May 1648 with the *Peace of Munster*.

And while these negotiations were going on, there was still fighting. In fact, the last major battle, the *Siege of Prague* was in progress when the final peace treaty was signed. On learning of the treaty, the Swedes withdrew from Prague, but not before looting the immense art collection that was in *Prague Castle*. Some historians even claim that the purpose of the siege of

Prague was mainly to obtain this collection, which even today, to the shame of the Swedes, has not been returned to the rightful owner.

1.3 The First Thirty Years War: 1618-1648

The War's Legacy

Until the World Wars of the 20th century, this war ranks as the most destructive in the history of Europe. Since most of the fighting and foreign occupation occurred in the German states, it was here where most destruction of property and loss of life occurred. In addition to the disruption of the war itself, there were other factors that contributed to the destruction and de-population of central Europe.

And it wasn't just the ravages caused by the armies, nature lent a hand and produced, especially in the 1630's, some of the coldest winters Europe had ever seen. This resulted in the shortening of the growing season in much of central Europe, which along with the devastation of farms by the roving bands of solders and brigands, caused famine and more suffering.

This was the time of the little ice age, and especially during the 1630's, Europe experienced extreme cold and shortened growing seasons that caused wide-spread famine. Here are a couple of examples illustrating the extreme weather suffered during this time. For example, in 1635, the Upper Rhine River froze at Speyer and, in 1638, in southern France, the Marseilles harbor froze.

The initial alignments, in the 1620's, were mostly along confessional lines, but as the war continued in to the 1630's and beyond, other issues such as economic, political, and cultural began to replace confessional alignment.

Evidence for this shift to nationalistic motives is illustrated by the fact that not all belligerents remained faithful to one side or the other. Several switched sides once and one switched sides twice. Savoy, Denmark, Brandenburg, and France switched once, while Saxony switched twice. This is another strong indicator that confessional considerations were not primary for, at least, some participants.

Late in the war, the protestant states of Saxony, Brandenburg, and Denmark switched to the Emperor's side, while the Catholic state France fought on the protestant side because the anti-Hapsburg sentiments within France superseded their Catholic faith.

Although, confessional differences seem to have lessened over the course of the war, religious sentiments were still very strong when compared to the decline in religious fervor that exists in Europe today. This war can reasonably be considered the last of the western religious wars, even though it had strong secular components that became more prominent as the war progressed. Today, it is only in the East where the nascent extreme Islam has asserted itself where we find open religiously motivated warfare both internecinal and external.

Without doubt, this war ranks as one of those that truly changed the history of Europe, and, by extension, the history of most of the world. The destruction and human misery caused by the almost continuous open warfare over a period of thirty years was unprecedented until the World Wars.

Even during the periods when no major battles were fought, the opposing armies still relied on pillage for sustenance and other provisions, which resulted in vast regions being stripped of crops and livestock that were needed by the local inhabitants for survival

Conditions in much of central Europe became so bad that it became one of those rare times when conditions are so atrocious that the culture responsible for this conflict finally changed, at least, for a while.

Small wonder that after thirty years of this devastation, along with the natural issues, that the belligerents were more than ready to seek peace and decided that religious co-existence was the better than killing each other in what after a generation of fighting, must have seemed like an endless process.

There seems little doubt that by the year 1648, the destruction of life and property in central Europe was such that recovery would take not years, but generations. It has even been claimed with some validity that it wasn't until the 19th century and the beginnings of Germanic unification by the Prussians that central Europe can be said to have recovered.

1.3 The First Thirty Years War: 1618-1648

1.4 Custer's Last Battle

Reconsidering Custer's Last Battle…

Preface

Given that there have been Custer books and essays without number, why would anyone want to write another one? That, of course, is a good question, and I hope to have a good answer.

After a visit to the battle site, I discovered that most of what I was taught in school – primary and secondary – was either incomplete or wrong. Even with all of the enormous bibliography on Custer, most people still have wrong and incomplete ideas about what actually happened, and they have no idea of why it happened.

And that is why I began to research the battle and see what the most popular, and most recent, authors have had to say. It seems that older texts tend to favor Custer and blame Reno and Benteen for the disaster, while more recent publications are more mixed, but still often biased either for or against Custer.

In any case, most take a contingency or *what if* attitude and often make assumptions about what happened. I have tried to avoid both assumptions and conjectures, and for the most part I believe I have been successful. I did find it necessary or expediant to use the word probable or probably a few times, but this does not change the validity of my thesis.

1.4 Custer's Last Battle

Background: Custer at the Washita

On the 27th of November 1868, George Armstrong Custer[45] at the head of the US 7th Regiment of Cavalry perpetrated a dawn attack against a village of Cheyenne Indians camped along the Washita River in western Indian Territory. This group of Cheyenne, supposedly under the protection of the US Army, were on a reservation, and even had a white flag posted as a sign of their non-belligerency.

This went either unnoticed or ignored by GAC[46], who as usual, was only interested in an easy fight and, at this time, he was particularly interested in the rehabilitation of his public image. He needed both, because only months earlier, he had been court-martialed for desertion and the mistreatment of soldiers under his command. Found guilty of both charges, he was sentenced to a one-year suspension without pay. However, again GAC's good fortune held and within a few months, he was reinstated.

In any case, just before dawn, the unsuspecting village was attacked and most of the fighting was over within minutes. Over the next few hours following the short and one-sided fight, the village was destroyed, and hundreds of Indian horses were killed. Although, the troopers suffered few casualties, over one hundred Indians were killed, including women and children, and by early afternoon, GAC began planning his withdrawal, which included about 50 Indian women and children hostages.

In this encounter, Custer's fortune again held, but this time just barely. Because he did not do a reconnaissance, he did not know that only a short distance down the Washita River was a much larger Cheyenne village from which hundreds of warriors emerged in pursuit. GAC's troopers soon found themselves heavily outnumbered, but because of the hostages, the newly arrived Cheyenne warriors held back from what might have been a devastating attack.

Realizing that he was in a desperate situation, GAC used a feint that tricked the Indians into believing that he was moving to attack the larger village, but as soon as it was dark, he reversed his march and managed to get away.

---

[45] During the US Civil War, George Armstrong Custer achieved the rank of Brevet Major General, but following the war he, like many others, reverted to his permanent Army rank of Lieutenant Colonel. He fought through four years of the Civil War and because of his luck, reckless courage, and desire for publicity, he became famous throughout the country.

[46] For convenience, I will use mostly use GAC for George Armstrong Custer.

As mentioned above, overall, he had suffered light casualties with the worse being that of an isolated group of troopers under the command of a Major Elliott. This group of 20 troopers, isolated from the main body, found themselves heavily outnumbered by hostiles, and all were killed. This incident prompted a certain Capt. Frederick Benteen[47] to accuse GAC of abandoning Elliott, and GAC never forgot or forgave the criticism.

Once again, the good fortune that had brought him safely through the Civil War was still with him. No doubt he and his supporters believed that this luck would surely continue. The unprovoked fight at the Washita was proclaimed a victory and his reputation was made once again.

GAC's justification (or excuse) for the killing was that the village contained men guilty of murder, theft, and other outrages. Stephen Ambrose put this into perspective when in his book *Crazy Horse and Custer*, he stated 'Denver was also full of men guilty of murder, theft, and other outrages, but the Army never thought about shooting up and burning down Denver'![48]

---

[47] Captain Frederick Benteen was a regular Army officer who had held the rank of Brevet Brigadier General during the US Civil War.

[48] Stephen Ambrose, *Crazy Horse and Custer*, (New York: Anchor Books, 1996), 324.

1.4 Custer's Last Battle

Considering the Battle

As a child, like most children even today, I was taught that the cause of George Armstrong Custer's annihilation was the disobedience of orders by certain officers in his command. It is also commonly thought that the entire 7th Regiment was wiped out and that the hostile warriors numbered in the thousands. For example, even as recently as 2015, a book review in the New York Times stated that GAC and the entire 7th Regiment killed. Of course, these are just a few of the myths about the Little Bighorn Battle that have persisted.

Over the years, besides the voluminous written works, numerous paintings depicting the battle were produced that show GAC clustered with his loyal men, surrounded by masses of Indians, and invariably they all show him in a heroic stance. This image, of the so-called *Last Stand*, factual or not, has persisted over the years and will probably persist well into the future.

This is because, in the USA, we like our heroes to be larger than life, and GAC's image certainly fits the pattern. Although in recent years, there is some tarnish on that image. Increased awareness, seasoned with political correctness, has caused many to question what GAC and the rest of the Army were up to in the first place. It cannot be denied that the native tribes were defending their homeland against the incursion of settlers and trying to preserve their nomadic way of life.

Even so, there are still plenty of individuals and groups that are actively keeping the *Custer Myth* alive. This has been true since the beginning when his widow, Elizabeth *'Libby'* Bacon Custer, began a 50 plus year crusade to keep her husband's heroic image firmly planted in the US gallery of heroes.[49]

Like all myths and legends, the *Custer Myth* is partial truth mingled with falsehood and exaggeration, and like all myths, separating myth from truth is, at best, difficult.

Although, GAC's bravery in battle is well documented, it cannot be denied that he was impetuous and known to lack discipline. He was also a blatant self-promoter who wrote anonymous articles for journals and newspapers about his great exploits. Some true, all embellished.

---

[49] Libby died in 1933.

So much has been written about GAC's personality and his exploits, such that I feel that it is not necessary to go into the details. His record at West Point (poor), the Civil War (good to excellent) and fighting Indians (mixed) is well known. The literature is full of stories about his personal traits, both good and bad. Brash, ambitious, impetuous, arrogant, experienced, and extremely self-confident are probably enough of a description. If the reader feels anything was left out, please add your own.

1.4 Custer's Last Battle

Reconsidering the Battle

In reconsidering this battle, the objective herein is to show how the course of events unfolded on that fateful day, June 25th, 1876, and whether results could (or should) have been different. Motives, morality, and so on are beyond the scope of this essay. That is, the focus is on determining, as accurately as possible, what actually happened and why it happened that way.

The Plan: June 1876

General Philip Sheridan, commander of the Military Division of the Missouri, had a grand plan that he and General Alfred Terry, commander of the Dakota Military Department, had developed to defeat the bands of Sioux[50] Indians that had left their reservations and were considered by the US government to be renegades. This plan called for three forces to converge in what is now south-central Montana and through battle or other means force the Sioux back to their reservations.

The first of these three forces, which proceeded from Fort Abraham Lincoln in Dakota Territory under the command of Gen. Terry, had a force, of just over 900 men. This force included the 7th US Cavalry Regiment under the command of Lt. Col. G. Custer.[51] After leaving Fort Lincoln, this force was to proceed west to the Yellowstone River, then move up the Yellowstone to the mouth of Rosebud Creek, which is only a short distance from the mouth of the Bighorn River.

At the same time, the second force, under the command of Col. John Gibbon, with about 500 men, advanced east from Fort Ellis, in western Montana Territory, down the Yellowstone River to link up with Terry's force at or near the mouth of the Bighorn River. The third force of about 1300 cavalry and infantry, under General George Crook, commander of the Platte Department, advanced north from Fort Fetterman, located near present day Douglas, Wyoming, toward the head waters of the Rosebud Creek.

---

[50] Although most of the Indians that were later encountered were from various branches of the Sioux, small groups from other tribes, such as the Cheyenne, were also present. For convenience, I will use either Indians or Sioux in references to the assembled tribes.

[51] GAC was the acting commander of the 7th US Cavalry. The actual commander, Colonel Samuel Sturgis, was on detached duty in Saint Louis.

The goal of these three forces was to meet on or about the 26th of June and, hopefully, trap the Sioux at a place unspecified in the orders from Gen. Sheridan. That is, Gen. Sheridan's orders did not specify exactly how they expected to meet or exactly where. Given the lack of ability to easily communicate with each other and other factors such as little knowledge of the terrain to be crossed, the chance of all three meeting on the 26th seems remote. And, of course, there is always the unexpected!

Crook Meets the Unexpected

Sure enough, on the 17th of June, the Crook force did indeed encounter the unexpected. This force, having advanced north without incident from Fort Fetterman, was at this time located near the head waters of Rosebud Creek, awoke on the morning of the 17th to what seemed to be another typical day on the march. Then about 0800[52], while most of the troops were still lounging around after a leisurely breakfast, they started to hear gunfire coming from north of their position.

At first, many thought it was just some of the Indians scouts shooting game, but when it started to intensify it became obvious that something else was going on. And sure enough, within minutes, the scouts, who had left the camp at dawn to scout to the north, came riding in hard and fast with Sioux hostiles in hot pursuit!

Within minutes, a full-scale battle was under way between Crook's troops and the Sioux. This fight, with much maneuvering by both sides, lasted through the morning without either side gaining an advantage and without a lot of damage being done to either side.

By 1330 (1:30PM) the fighting was over with the Sioux withdrawing to the north and Crook's force withdrawing to the southeast. Crook's excuse for his withdrawal was lack of supplies, especially ammunition. It seems that although there were few casualties, the Army had managed to expend more than 25,000 cartridges.

The significance of this encounter is that the Indians were more aggressive than the Army had previously experienced. It was the first time that, instead of scattering to avoid pursuit or capture, the Sioux had not only

---

[52] In the interest of clarity, I have chosen to use 24-hour clock notation (aka military time) throughout this essay. The timeline, during the last few hours of the Little Bighorn Battle, is easier to follow and understand with this convention. Hopefully this convention will not be an inconvenience.

stood and fought but had offensively started the fight against a large command of more than 1000 men!

This was big news, but for some reason, Crook did not make any attempt to notify Terry about the encounter. He did not even write his report until two days after the fight and then it was only sent to Gen. Sheridan in Chicago. By the time, Gen. Sheridan received the report, June 23rd, GAC was into his second day of approach to the Little Bighorn and out of communication with Terry or any other army units.

The First Day: June 22, 1876

At noon on June the 22nd, 1876, GAC and the 12 companies of the U. S. 7th Cavalry (652 men) separated from the rest of Terry's command and began their fateful journey to the Little Bighorn River in what is now south-central Montana. Their mission was to ride up to the head waters of Rosebud Creek and cross over to the west and then descend the Little Bighorn and link up with the Terry-Gibbon force.

Although Custer's orders from General Terry contained some general guidelines and recommendations, they were imprecise and left Custer with a lot of room for personal discretion. Whether this was due to confidence in Custer or reluctance by Terry to be precise is not known, but the result is that Terry's written orders clearly gave Custer considerable freedom of interpretation.[53]

Anyway, before separating, there was a conversation between Terry and GAC where, according to witnesses, Terry told GAC not to be greedy and save some Indians for us. To which he replied, "No I won't." This piece of ambiguity nicely illustrates the relationship between the two, and who was the cat and who the mouse.

Those who knew Custer, seemed to have one of two opinions. Those who were unquestionably on his side, and those who could not abide him with varying degrees of dislike. Of course, Custer could not abide anyone who did not idolize him. Accordingly, there was among the officers of the regiment, those who were Custer insiders and those on the outside.

---

[53] See Appendix A for a copy of General Terry's orders to Custer.

The most notable of these outsiders were Major Marcus Reno[54] and Captain Frederick Benteen (mentioned earlier about his criticism of GAC at the Washita). This division was apparently a source of much friction within the regiment and, as we shall see, apparently had influence on some of Custer's actions during these final days

On that first day, away from higher authority, Custer was in his element. Independent command was what he lived for more than anything else except his wife, Libby. Because of the late start, the column only made 12 miles that first day, just enough for Custer to be on his own and out of the reach of Terry.

Now that he was independent, he wasted no time in rearranging the regiment so that all company commanders reported directly to him. This meant that the second highest ranking officer, Major Reno, effectively, had no job within the regiment. As mentioned, Reno was not a Custer-man.

The Second Day: June 23, 1876
Having only progressed 12 miles on the first day, the column was up and on the road by 0500. This day was uneventful, except that during the day there was an increase in recent Indian sign.[55] They made 33 uneventful miles up the Rosebud that day before settling in for a restful night.

The Third Day: 0500 June 24 - 1200 June 25th
Again, on the 24th, the column was on the march at 0500 and continued for an hour and a half when they stopped to inspect the remnants of a recent Sioux camp. This stop was at the place where, only days before, Sitting Bull, Sioux spiritual leader, had performed a Sun Dance.

This Sun Dance was especially significant since it was this Sun Dance that gave Sitting Bull a vision of falling soldiers, which the Sioux interpreted as a sign of a victory over the soldiers. A few days after the Sun Dance, it was this same band of Sioux that had fought Crook's force to a draw.

---

[54] Major Marcus Reno reached the rank of Brevet Brigadier General during the Civil War and, like other breveted officers, reverted to his permanent rank of Major after the war.

[55] For example, Indian sign include such things as tracks of the hundreds of ponies, the scratch marks of the travois, camp debris, and well grazed grass.

1.4 Custer's Last Battle

It was also at this stop where another event occurred which might have been interpreted as an ill omen for GAC's command. It seems that officer's call was sounded and, to indicate his position, GAC's red and blue swallow-tail pennant was stuck in the ground.

Almost immediately a gust of wind blew the pennant to the ground. Again, the pennant was stuck into the ground and again it blew down pointing in the direction from which they had come. Finally, Lt. Godfrey[56], who was standing close by, took the pennant, and wedged it in a sagebrush bush where it held firm.[57]

After resuming the march over increasingly difficult ground, they halted for the night about 1945 at a location that later became known as the Busby Bend of the Rosebud. At this point the approximate distance covered by the column, over the three days, was 72 miles (12 on the 22nd, 33 on the 23rd, and 27 on the 24th).

Like the day before, this day showed more evidence of recent Indian activity, including indication that the Indians before them were more numerous than had been anticipated.

Witnesses noted that GAC was more serious than usual, and there were none of the hijinks that GAC and his brothers normally engaged in when on the march.[58] This, along with increasing Indian sign, combined to make this march seem different to many of the veterans of other GAC campaigns.

This was especially true among the Indian scouts[59] who began to worry about the number of Sioux they were following. The scouts had also noticed that as the day's march progressed, tracks indicated that more bands of Sioux were joining the main group.

---

[56] Lt. Godfrey survived the battle and eventually rose to the rank of Brigadier General. He was also a leading supporter of Custer's legacy and a sharp critic of Reno and Benteen.

[57] Such incidents have a long history of being considered bad omens. For example, a similar one occurred on 22 August 1642 when at the start of the English Civil War, England's King Charles I had his banner planted as a rallying point for his supporters. Twice the banner was blown to the ground. Seven years later, Charles had not only lost the war, but also his head.

[58] GAC was accompanied by both his older brother Captain Tom Custer, commander of C Company and his younger brother Boston Custer, who had come along as a civilian observer. They both perished in the coming fight.

[59] The scouts included more than 30 Arikara (Ree) scouts and six Crow scouts. The Crow scouts were especially important, because they were scouting on familiar tribal lands.

Shortly after the evening halt, several advance scouts came riding in. They informed GAC that the Sioux had turned west and taken the route from the Rosebud that would carry them over the divide to the Little Bighorn River. After considering this latest information, GAC decided to send Lt. Charles Varnum, the officer in charge of the scouts, ahead with a few of the scouts and an interpreter to see if they could locate the hostile camp.

Accordingly, at 2120, Lt. Varnum and the scouts rode off to find the high point now called the Crow's Nest. In the dark, this eleven-mile trip turned out to be a five-and-a-half-hour journey.[60] Even so, they arrived about an hour before sunrise and had to wait an hour before it was light enough for observation.

With the breaking dawn, the Crow scouts in the group claimed that they could see what they said was an exceptionally large pony herd, perhaps 12 or 13 miles away. These scouts also claimed to see the smoke from scores of cooking fires that marked the location of the hostile camp.

Varnum claimed that, because of the hazy atmosphere, he could not see the herd or the smoke even with the binoculars that he had. But having faith in the scouts, he wrote out a note for GAC and gave it to two of the Ree (Arikara) scouts. It was now 0520 on the 25th.

During this time, shortly after midnight (0030), GAC rousted out the command after only four hours' rest and had them on the march. They continued up Rosebud Creek and took the Davis Creek branch, which leads west to the divide, and was the path taken by the Sioux only a few days earlier.

Some writers have interpreted this move as a violation of Terry's orders, but it probably was not, given his order's vagueness. Anyway, after a march of about seven miles, GAC halts the column to await word from Varnum. It was now 0315 and, as it turned out, GAC still had to wait over four hours, which was lost time even though it allowed the men and horses to rest.

Finally, at 0730, the Ree scouts from Varnum finally arrived with the note for GAC. After reading the note, GAC delayed any action until 0800 when

---

[60] The Crows scouts knew this country well, it and is still Crow country.

1.4 Custer's Last Battle

he decided to ride to the Crow's nest and have a look. His trip to the Crow's Nest took an hour and he stayed at the lookout until 1020.[61]

Apparently, while at the Crow's Nest, the scouts were not able to convince GAC about either the size or the location of the Sioux camp. Consequently, GAC had a difficult time deciding what to do. In the meantime, Reno, or someone else, decided to move closer to the divide and so the main column proceeded, from this first halt on the 25th, four miles closer to the divide.[62]

At this point GAC called the officers together to review the situation and to decide on future action. Again, this took time and the column did not move again until 1145, and even then, they only proceeded about a mile before stopping again just after they had crossed the divide (Halt 3

---

[61] Why it took the Ree scouts two hours to deliver the note, when GAC made the reverse trip in an hour has never been adequately explained.

[62] When GAC returned from the lookout he was annoyed at the move of the regiment, but because there seemed some confusion about who had ordered the move, nothing was done about it.

The Last Hours: June 25 - 1200 to 2100

Noon on the 25th signals the start of the timeline, which is critical in understanding what, when, where, and why events unfolded the way they did.

Although over the years, there has been much debate about the timeline of events, there now appears to be a consensus among most who have studied the battle, and it is this timeline that will be followed here.[63] This timeline, like all timelines of complex and dramatic events, has a margin of error, but it is accurate enough to show how events unfolded and to follow the sequence of events that day.

As mentioned above, it seems that GAC had doubts about even the presence of a camp and did not believe the scouts that spoke of an exceptionally large pony herd – the largest they had ever seen! In fact, eye witnesses claim that, even after his return from the Crow's Nest, GAC and the scouts argued about both the exact location and size of the Sioux camp.

The scouts also claimed that the column had been seen such that the village would be alerted about the troopers' presence and that GAC should attack immediately. Finally, GAC accepted their advice and decided to advance at once.[64]

The First Big Mistake

While at Halt 3, GAC issued his final officer's call and made his fateful decision to divide the eleven companies of the main column up into three battalions. Although both Reno and Benteen were disliked by GAC, by virtue of their seniority, they were each given command of one of the battalions.

The companies were divided such that Reno was assigned three companies (A, G, and M - 175 men); Benteen was assigned three companies (D, H, and K - 120 men); and GAC retained direct command of five companies (C, E, F, I, and L - 221 men).

The twelfth company, B company, was escorting the pack train along with an extra 6 or 7 troopers from each of the other companies. This brought the

---

[63] For a detailed timeline see: John S. Gray, *Custer's Last Campaign*, (Lincoln, University of Nebraska Press, 1991).

[64] It should be mentioned that the Sioux were traditional enemies of both the Crows and the Arikara. This could explain their eagerness for the troopers to attack.

1.4 Custer's Last Battle

total number of men with the pack train to about 136 or just over 20% of the total force.

Within minutes of making these assignments, about 1200, the GAC and Reno battalions continued westerly, down what later became known as Reno Creek, toward the Little Bighorn River. At the same time, GAC, inexplicably, sent Benteen and his three companies on a roundabout detour to the southwest. This move put Benteen out of contact with the other two battalions, which would delay any possible linkup with other elements of the command. This was GAC's first big mistake.

The assignment of battalions was not a mistake, the mistake was the sending of Benteen off on his own, which subsequently led to the physical separation of the four command elements. This had the effect of delaying Benteen's movement to the Little Big Horn river and assured that his three companies would be separated from the other two battalions. It should be noted that by this time, the slower moving pack train had already fallen behind.

GAC's excuse for sending Benteen off on a detour was to determine if any of the Indians were moving south from the Little Bighorn valley, but more likely it was an excuse to get rid of Benteen. Either way, it was a task more suited to the scouts who moved faster, and with more stealth, than three companies of cavalry.

With Benteen off on his wild goose chase, GAC and Reno continued down Reno Creek. After proceeding eight miles down Reno Creek, GAC and Reno arrived where only a lone tepee was left of what had been a recent Sioux camp. It was now 1415, and while pausing to inspect the tepee, GAC received, from the scouts, a report that the Sioux seemed to be running away.

However, this report was an error, what the scouts had seen was a small band of Indian stragglers rushing to catchup with the main camp. What influence this had on GAC's future actions is impossible to determine, except apparently it did cause GAC to increase the pace of both his and Reno's battalions.

The location of the Lone Tepee is important as a check-point for each of the four contingents of troopers. As shown in Chart-1 (page 92), at 1512, an hour after GAC and Reno, Benteen passed the Lone Tepee, but the pack train did not get there until twenty minutes after Benteen.

After an advance of twelve miles from Halt 3, GAC and Reno arrived at Ford A, where Reno Creek enters the Little Bighorn (see Chart 1). This took about three hours and it was now almost 1500.

At this point, GAC still did not know exactly where the Sioux were located, and he did not know their numbers, consequently, prior to proceeding, GAC should have sent some of the scouts ahead to observe the exact location and size of the village. Instead, he chose to once again split his command by sending Reno off independently to attack the camp.

The Second Big Mistake
Just prior to reaching the Little Bighorn, Reno was told, not by GAC himself, but by Custer's adjutant, Lt. Cooke, that he was to cross Ford A to the west side of the Little Bighorn and attack the south end of the Sioux camp, which was still about 3 miles away. Cooke also told Reno that GAC would support Reno with the 'whole outfit.'[65] This hasty decision to send Reno across the Little Bighorn was taken before GAC had any idea of the size of the Indian camp.

From Ford A, only the southern end of the camp could be seen with the bulk of the camp remaining unseen beyond the first cluster of tepees. By sending Reno off into the valley, GAC's forces were now divided into four isolated elements.

Given the lack of knowledge of the hostiles dispositions and numbers, precipitously sending in Reno into the valley was irresponsible and violated basic military principles (Such as, lack of reconnaissance and division of forces when enemy strength and dispositions are unknown). This was GAC's second big mistake.

Side Comment on Number of Warriors: Over the years, there have been many estimates made about the size of the camp and the number of warriors in the camp. The one thing most of these have in common is the exaggerated number of tepees and number of warriors. Estimates range from 1000 to more than 6000 warriors and with a correspondingly wide range for the number of tepees. The more accurate estimates are those at the lower end and probably did not exceed 1100-1200 warriors, and even this number is probably generous.[66]

---

[65] Of course, at this point, the pack train and Benteen's battalion were already separated from GAC and Reno.

[66] This number is based on the count of tepee marks left after the Indian camp moved on.

1.4 Custer's Last Battle

First Contact: 1500 to 1610 Hours

At Ford A, Reno took his battalion over the river into the Little Bighorn valley and advanced north at a trot. After a two-mile advance and still about a mile from the south end of the camp, Reno was confronted by hundreds of hostiles moving south from the village. It immediately became obvious that the Sioux were not retreating, rather they were advancing to fight. Custer's adjutant Lt. Cooke, who had accompanied Reno into the valley, now left and reported back to GAC that the Indians were not running as expected. *This was GAC's first confirmation that the hostiles were standing and fighting.*

As the Indians closed in and the shooting started, Reno dismounted his troopers and formed a skirmish line. This action, which was standard cavalry procedure, had the effect of reducing his strength by about 25% because when the troopers are dismounted, one in four men are designated horse holders.[67] This action started at 1518 and continued past 1530.

Shortly after Reno's troopers started fighting in the valley, GAC had a second confirmation that the Sioux were fighting when he was briefly observed on the bluffs east of the river. It was also clear that GAC was moving to the north, away from Reno and the rest of his command.

On seeing firsthand that the hostiles were standing and fighting instead of running away, GAC was once again confronted with a decision point and should have revised his plans. Instead, he continued to widen the gap between his battalion and the rest of the regiment.

It should be recalled, that Reno had been told that GAC would back up his attack with the whole outfit. However, on seeing GAC on the eastern bluffs and his continued movement to the north, it was obvious that this was not the case and Reno was on his own. Whether it was the pressure from the Indians, the thought of being abandoned, or some other reason that caused Reno to withdraw we will never know. In any case, withdraw he did.

It is here that we will leave Reno and his men and check in on GAC, Benteen, and the pack train.

---

[67] This practice dates from the Civil War where it was customary for the US Cavalry to fight dismounted. A major difference is that from 1863 to the end of the war in 1865, most US Cavalry troopers were armed with the extra fire-power of repeaters, instead of the single shot Springfield's used at the Little Bighorn Battle. Why the US Cavalry regressed after the Civil War is strange but with the reduction of the trooper's firepower, use of the horse holders seems hard to justify

We know that GAC advanced north along the eastern bluffs and at 1530 or so he was at or near the location later called Weir Point. We also know that at 1515 GAC sent Sgt. Kanipe to the rear with a verbal message for the pack train to hurry and not stop for any lost packs.

Sending this message can be interpreted that, GAC knew not only that the Indians were fighting instead of fleeing, but he also knew the camp was much larger than expected. For reasons, we do not know, just minutes after sending the first messenger, GAC decided to send a second messenger and had his adjutant Cooke write out a note for Benteen to hurry and to bring up ammunition packs. This note was given to trooper John Martin at 1532.[68]

Side Comment: Reno started his retreat to the bluffs about 1530. At that time, GAC was at Weir Point, the Pack Train was seven miles behind Custer at the Lone Tepee, and Benteen still on route to Ford A, was about four or more miles behind Custer. Put simply, Custer had scattered his regiment over a width of about seven miles such that none of the four elements were in contact with any other.

With hard riding, the first messenger, Sgt. Kanipe, reached at 1542. At this time, Benteen was a mile and a half from the lone tepee and 40 minutes from reaching Reno Hill. After a brief meeting with Benteen, Sgt. Kanipe rides on, meets the pack train, and delivers the hurry-up message at 1548. The pack train was then more than an hour and a half from reaching Reno Hill, which means that the pack train was more than two hours from GAC's current position.

At the time GAC sent Martin with the Benteen note, Reno was still fighting in the valley west of the river, Benteen was three plus miles to GAC's rear, and the pack train was more than eight miles behind GAC, and he must have realized that given the slow movement of the pack train and Benteen's roundabout, Benteen and the pack train would not be in contact with each other.

If GAC knew that he needed reinforcements, why did he continue to widen the gap between his battalion and the rest of the command such that reuniting the command was becoming increasingly problematic?

---

[68] Another unanswered question is why was this note addressed to Benteen? GAC and his command, at that time, would not have known if Benteen was in contact or even close to the pack train.

1.4 Custer's Last Battle

He also knew that the pack train traveled at about half the speed of the unencumbered troopers, and, therefore, he must have known that any resupply of ammunition was still miles behind. At 1532, when Martin was sent with the note, the pack train, making only about 2 to 3 miles per hour, was at or near the Lone Tepee, which meant that the pack train was, at least, seven miles (or more than two hours) behind GAC.

Apparently, GAC made no attempt to contact Reno at any time and had no intention of supporting Reno as he said he would. Since we know that two messengers Knape and Martin), several stragglers, and Boston Custer[69] safely traversed the region between GAC's command and as far south as the pack train, is seems that a message to Reno could have been sent.

Reno and Benteen Consolidate:1610 to 1725 Hours

At 1610, Reno, after a chaotic retreat from the valley, had managed to reach a defensible position on the eastern bluffs. Unfortunately, by this time his battalion had suffered more than 30 men killed, a dozen wounded, and more than a dozen men were still trapped west of the river in the woods that Reno had just left.

This reduced Reno's battalion to just over 100 troopers. Additionally, on reaching Reno Hill, Reno's men and horses were exhausted and in no shape to immediately take any offensive action.

Fortunately, only ten minutes after Reno's arrival, Benteen and his three companies arrived with much needed material and moral support. Within minutes after Benteen's arrival, several volleys of gun fire were heard coming from the north. It was now 1625.

Although the sound of these volleys confirmed that GAC was engaged with the hostiles, there was still no definite knowledge of his whereabouts. All they had was the note for Benteen to bring up ammunition packs, and the pack train was still an hour away from arrival at Reno Hill.

It could be argued that GAC's tracks would be easy to follow, but they still needed to wait for the pack train. Now Reno and Benteen were faced with the choice of either advancing to the sound of the fighting or waiting for the pack train.

---

[69] Custer's younger brother, Boston, had been traveling with the pack train, but he left the train at 1417and managed to catch up with Custer's battalion at 1549.

In any case, after some discussion, most officers agreed that they should stay where they were until the pack train arrived or until they heard from GAC. Not only were the supplies important, but the additional 100 plus troopers escorting the pack train would be a welcome reinforcement that would bring the Reno-Benteen contingent up to seven companies with more than 350 men. Waiting for the pack train was a better choice than rushing off into an unknown situation, it was the correct military decision.[70]

The Weir Point Advance and Return

After 25 or 30 minutes of waiting and hearing gunfire from the north, one of the company commanders, Lt. Weir of D company, grew impatient and since from Reno Hill they had no visual contact with GAC, without asking permission, he mounted up and proceeded north to see if he could learn anything about GAC and events to the north.

The second in command of Weir's company thought that he was supposed to follow Weir with the whole company, so he had D company mount and proceeded to follow Weir. It was now 1705.

So, off they went for about a mile until they came to a high point, that, not surprisingly, later became known as Weir Point. Shortly after leaving Reno Hill, Weir and D company heard a few more volleys of gunfire from the north. As it turned out, these were the last. After these last volleys, only uncoordinated gunfire was heard. It was now 1710.

Apparently reconsidering the decision to wait for the pack train, Benteen, without consulting Reno, decided to follow Weir with the other two companies in his battalion and M company from Reno's battalion.

At 1725, Lt. Weir and D company arrived at Weir Point where, about three miles north, they could see riders with guidons. At first, they thought were troopers from GAC's battalion. However, when observed through binoculars they saw a different picture.

With telescopic assistance, they discerned that what they were looking at were Indians with guidons riding around shooting at objects on the ground. The only possible conclusion was that the objects on the ground were some of GAC's troopers!

---

[70] Some say that the correct choice is always to march to the sound of the guns, but this is an over simplification and certainly does not apply in all cases.

1.4 Custer's Last Battle

Comments on Artifacts and Testimonies

In 1984, there was a grass fire at the Little Bighorn National Monument that burned off the vegetation covering a large portion of the Custer battle area (Map-1, page 93). This gave archeologists a unique opportunity to look for battle remnants using visual observation, facilitated by the burnt off grass, and metal detectors, which could effectively locate metal objects buried several inches in the ground.

This effort produced a substantial number of artifacts which together with another metal detector survey in 2004 gave new insight into the flow of battle. Although the recovery of these artifacts sounds promising, there are several issues that place some doubt on the reliability of many of these artifacts.

A major problem is that over the years, and especially during the early years after the battle, souvenir hunters are estimated to have removed hundreds or even thousands of artifacts. Given that and other considerations, I have chosen to mostly ignore all battle artifacts except Indian bullets.

The reasons for this is that other objects, such as cartridge cases and other artifacts lying around on the ground are easy to pick up, while the bullets were imbedded in the ground and out of sight. Plus, for the most part, it is easy to differentiate, bullets from Indian weapons and those from trooper weapons.

Although, it should be noted that, while the battle was still active, a small number of Indians were likely to have armed themselves with the guns of fallen troopers, these bullets do not greatly influence the overall picture. The distribution of Indians bullets is shown in Map-3 (page 95).

In determining GAC's annihilation scenario, in addition to the Indian bullets found on the battle field, I have also relied on testimony of individual Sioux and Cheyenne participants, the Crow scout Curley, and the distribution of grave-markers.

The first of these, the Sioux and Cheyenne participants, have somewhat confusing accounts of what happened. They seem to have had little sense of chronological order and where something happened. Still, their testimonies, cautiously considered, provide useful information about events.

The Crow scout, Curley, claimed that he was hidden under a Sioux blanket and saw the whole battle. Unfortunately, Curley gave several versions of what happened and some of the other scouts claim he had left for home and did not see anything.[71]

As for the artifacts, as stated above, I have essentially ignored all artifacts except Indian bullets. This is because the bullets are the artifacts most likely not to have been disturbed and, therefore, the most reliable.

Lastly, I considered the actual and presumed locations of the troopers who were killed. Although there are errors in some grave-marker locations, they are accurate enough to provide a general pattern of the action that annihilated GAC's battalion. In addition to the markers themselves, there is the testimony of those who either did the initial burials or participated in the reburials a couple of years later has been considered.

Custer's actions from 1530 to 1730 June 25th

Again, it is necessary to back up and try to piece together what happened to GAC and his battalion in the two-hour span from when last seen by Trp. Martin (1530) to the realization of the Reno-Benteen troopers at Weir Point that, at least, part of GAC's battalion appeared to have been killed by the Sioux (1730).

The evidence indicates that after being sighted on the bluffs (near or at Weir Point), GAC advanced another two miles to the head of the Medicine Tail Coulee (hereinafter MTC).[72] This move, which occurred about the same time that Reno was retreating to the high ground east of the LBH River, puts three miles between GAC's and the Reno and Benteen contingents, and even more distance from the pack train.

It appears obvious that this continuation to the north cannot be considered the act of someone who planned to coordinate with or support his other battalions.

GAC's movements north halted when they reached the head of MTC, where GAC again continues the fragmentation of his command when he divides his battalion into two *wings*. One wing of two companies (E, F)

---

[71] An excellent reference for testimonies is W. A. Grahams book: *The Custer Myth* (Bonanza Books, New York, 1953).

[72] See Chart-1 and Map-1 (pages 95 and 96).

1.4 Custer's Last Battle

under Captain Yates and the other three companies (C, I, L) under Captain Keogh,[73] these two being the senior captains within his battalion.

The wing under Yates is also known as the left-wing and the one under Keogh as the right-wing. This must be considered as another GAC mistake, but, by this time, he had created a situation that was probably already hopeless.

At 1549, Boston Custer, who had left the pack train, joins up with GAC at the head of MTC and surely must have informed his brother how far back were Benteen and the pack train. Minutes later, at 1600, the scouts Boyer and Curley, who had been left near Weir Point by GAC to observe Reno's action in the valley, rejoin GAC with the news that Reno had been routed and was moving across the river and up the bluffs.

Once again, GAC received news that should have prompted a change in his plans, but again he failed to modify his actions and continued to the north. It seems apparent that GAC still made no effort to communicate with the rest of his command, instead, he sent his left-wing (Capt. Yates, Cos. E and F) down MTC towards the river while GAC and the right-wing remained at the head of MTC.

After descending the MTC to the eastern bank of the river, the left-wing exchanged fire with the hostiles on the other side. Meanwhile, GAC and the right-wing moved farther north to an area that became known as Nye-Cartwright Ridge (Map-1, page 93) where they were spread out to provide support for the left-wing.

Shortly after the left-wing began exchanging fire with the hostiles on the other bank, the hostiles began crossing the river. This caused the left-wing to begin withdrawing to the bluffs by way of the Deep Coulee that branched off to the left from the bottom of MTC This is the time (1625) when volley firing, which was support fire from the right-wing, was heard at Reno Hill.

From the time Martin was sent with the Benteen note, until the left and right wings are reunited on Nye-Cartwright Ridge is almost an hour (1532 to 1630).

---

[73] Some authors say that this wing was commanded by GAC himself, which may be, since, as far as we can tell, he remained with this wing.

This episode was the critical hour that used up most of the time available for GAC to bring his forces together. Instead, he chose to ignore two thirds of his total force and continued north. Why he continued north after the start of his fight is a mystery that will never be answered.

On realizing that the hostiles were not running away, but were standing and fighting, the prudent and wise move would have been to return south to linkup with the other elements of his command. Instead, both wings moved somewhat north to what is now called Calhoun Hill (after the commanding officer of I Company, see Map-2, page 94). As is apparent from the number of Indian bullets recovered and the number of grave-markers that this was an area of sharp fighting.

As the fighting intensified, most of the troopers, that were still able, moved north from Calhoun Hill, across Custer Ridge (aka Battle Ridge), and on to Custer Hill. The pattern of bullets, along with the grave-markers clearly show that the final fighting was from Calhoun Hill, across Custer Ridge, Custer Hill, and finally down the Deep Ravine (aka South Skirmish Line) that descends from Custer Hill toward the River (Map-4 page 96). In any case, the fighting was over before 1730.

Reminder: The objective here is not to discuss GAC's fight in detail, but to determine how and why Custer's battalion was lost and whether Reno and/or Benteen could have made a difference, and whether GAC's movements were correct.[74]

June 25th: Reno Hill - 1725 to 2100 Hours

Finally, at 1725, the pack train arrive at Reno Hill. With the pack train arrival, Reno decided to move the pack train, the rest of his men, with the wounded being helped, to Weir Point. Meanwhile, shortly after 1730, Weir was joined by Benteen and the three companies that had advanced with Benteen. This put four companies (D, H, K, M) at Weir Point, with the other three (A, B, G) and the pack train advancing slowly toward Weir Point.

About this time, it became apparent to the troopers at Weir Point that the Indians were now advancing toward their position. In fact, the hostiles were advancing faster than they realized and within minutes the troopers were beginning to exchange long-range fire with the hostiles.

---

[74] As mentioned in the Preface, there are many detailed accounts of the fate of GAC's battalion. Most are too pro-Custer or too anti-Custer, with only a few offering a balanced account.

Realizing their position was precariously exposed, the troopers began to withdraw back south toward the more defensible position at Reno Hill. As they made their way back, they met Reno coming north. With news of the advancing Indians, Reno's contingent quickly reversed direction and all, but K company continued their way back to Reno Hill.

Company K provided a rear-guard for the rest of the group and managed to effectively slow up the Indian advance until all troopers were back at Reno Hill (1800 or shortly thereafter). Once back at Reno Hill they began preparing as best they could for the coming fight and, in short order, the hostiles were on them.

Side Comment: It should be noted, that during the movement back to Reno Hill, the Reno-Benteen contingent was joined by a dozen men from Reno's battalion who had been left hiding in the woods west of the river and two stragglers from GAC's battalion whose horses had given out. This is more evidence that the area between GAC and Reno Hill was mostly clear of hostiles and GAC could have communicated with Reno and Benteen and/or successfully withdrawn to the south.

After the hostiles closed in on Reno Hill, the fighting, mostly at long range, continued until dark (2100). By that time, most of the Indians had drifted away to their camp to join the celebration that was to continue late into the night.

The Reno-Benteen contingent had survived the day, but as they listened to the sounds of celebration coming from the camp, they surely must have spent a very long night thinking about what the morning would bring.

June 26: The Next Day at Reno Hill

After sunrise on the 26th, the Sioux again started the attack against the Reno-Benteen defense at Reno Hill. Although, improved overnight into a better defensive position, they still suffered casualties, mostly, from long range sniping.

This day, fighting continued sporadically until about mid-day when the Indians began to drift away, and by late afternoon the fighting was essentially over. That evening, around 1900, the troopers on Reno Hill saw the Sioux moving south up the Little Bighorn River valley toward the

Bighorn Mountains and away from General Terry's force that they knew was slowly advancing from the north.

Here ends the Reno-Benteen part of this tale, except for a later discussion about what Reno and/or Benteen could have done differently and whether there was any action that they could (or should) have taken that might have saved, at least, part of GAC's command.

1.4 Custer's Last Battle

Recapitulation

The big question has always been, could Reno and Benteen if they tried, have rescued GAC and his troopers? The short answer is no, but to see this it is necessary to review the timeline from 1500 to 1730, along with trooper movement and dispositions.

However, before reviewing the timeline, there are several things to keep in mind.

- Troopers had ridden more than 100 miles in three days.
- The horses were on short rations (little or no oats and the grass they passed over had been depleted by the vast Indian pony herd.)
- In the final 24 hours, the troopers (and horses) had little rest.
- The pack train was slow and poorly managed.
- There was no advanced scouting of the valley floor and the Indian camp.
- GAC did not know about the fight at Rosebud Creek and how the Indians fought with unusual aggressiveness.

These factors all contributed to the disaster. As with most disasters and accidents, there are always multiple contributing factors. However, a factor that must be considered as a major factor is the influence of GAC's personality, which is well documented, and must be considered a strong contributor to the disaster.

Particularly, the question of his relationship with his two senior officers, Reno and Benteen which we know was far from cordial. Did GAC purposely leave them out of the fight to ensure that he got full credit, or did he just not realize the danger to his battalion? Even though we will never know the reasons, we do know that his actions were in error and set up the disaster.

GAC knew that the 100 plus mules in the pack train could not advance as fast as the horse mounted troopers,[75] but he continued to advance to the north where he soon found himself isolated and attacked from multiple sides. Recall, that by the time Reno retreated to Reno Hill, GAC was three miles north and Benteen and the pack train even farther away from GAC.

---

[75] For example, between Halt 3 and Lone Tepee (eight miles), the pack train progressed only at about 2-3 miles per hour, while the Custer and Reno battalions covered the same distance at 7 miles per hour.

When GAC got to the head of MTC (1555), Reno and his troopers were struggling to reach a defensive position on the eastern bluffs and could not possibly come to GAC's aid even if Reno knew aid was needed, which, at that time, he did not know.

At MTC, GAC was without support and already deeply committed to the fight. His closest possible support was Reno and he was more than three miles away with exhausted men and horses. Besides, Reno had no clear idea of where GAC had gone except probably north along the bluffs east of the Little Bighorn River. Because his advance took him out of visual contact, GAC did not know the exact whereabouts of Reno, Benteen, or the pack train.

After discovery of the size of the hostile camp and being attacked at MTC, GAC should have returned south to link up with the rest of the command, instead he did the opposite, he moved even farther north, closely followed by the hostiles. This, of course, just made GAC's isolation greater and the situation even worse. Clearly, after the second messenger (Trooper Martin) was sent, it seems apparent that GAC had no intention of further contact with either the Reno-Benteen battalions or the pack train.

We need to recall that, beginning at 1200, GAC began the administrative and physical division of his forces. To do this where little or nothing is known about enemy dispositions or strength is a violation of a basic military axiom. Even though Custer apologists claim that he did so for valid reasons and reference the fight at the Washita as an example where this tactic of dispersal was successful.[76]

As discussed above he was lucky at the Washita where the fight had very different circumstances. It is possible that GAC was trying to duplicate his Washita success by capturing women and children as hostages that could be used to deter attacks by the warriors. If so, it does account for his determination to advance to the north end of the Indian camp where many non-combatants had been sent for safety.

If Reno, after reaching Reno Hill, had immediately advanced in the direction taken by GAC, his small command, which consisted of just over 100 troopers, would have been easily annihilated. Given the de-moralized

---

[76] Another famous example of a fatal division of forces is the Battle of Isandlwana in southern Africa during the 1879 Zulu War. Lord Chelmsford, commander of the British forces advancing into Zululand, split his forces without knowledge of enemy dispositions or strength and the result was the slaughter of more than 1000 British troops!

1.4 Custer's Last Battle

condition of men and exhausted horses, it was probably not possible to rally them sufficiently for offensive movement or even establish effective self-defense

Not only were the men of Reno's battalion exhausted, but they had used up much of their issued ammunition and needed the resupply that the pack train would bring.

Given that there was a distance, of four miles from Reno Hill to Custer Hill and given the rough terrain and the poor condition of men and horses it would have taken at least an hour. As mentioned, there is a high probability that Reno's battalion, reduced to about 100 troopers, would have met the same fate as Custer's battalion.

Even with the timely arrival of Benteen's battalion, if both battalions had immediately started to advance north, they would have been too late and most likely have found themselves in a comparable situation that GAC had gotten himself into.

That is, they would be out in the open and without the necessary resupply from the pack train. Also, they would have to leave a substantial detachment with the wounded or attempt to take the wounded with them, which would slow their advance.

Given the distances involved, the lack of meaningful communication from GAC, Reno and Benteen, in agreement with most of the other officers, made the correct decision in deciding to wait for the pack train that would not only provide food and ammunition, but a substantial reinforcement to their complement of troopers.

It was only by staying together and returning to the defensible position at Reno Hill that the Reno-Benteen contingent managed to hold off the hostiles and wait for the arrival of the rest of Terry's command.

GAC's series of mistakes accumulated and quickly reached the point of no recovery. *First*, he divided his forces into four components and sent Benteen off on his roundabout. *Second*, was his hasty decision to use Reno, as a diversion, to attack the south end of the camp. *Third*, was his insistence on continuing north away from the rest of the regiment. *Fourth*, was his division of his battalion into two wings, which apparently operated independently for some time allowing the hostiles to attack first one then the other. Sioux participants later testified that GAC's troopers seems tired and confused.

Fifth, GAC, apparently, made no attempt to communicate with Reno after Reno crossed over the Little Bighorn and started his attack. Even after GAC learned that Reno had been forced to withdraw back across the river and seek higher ground, he continued his northern movements without sending any messages to Reno,

Of the two messages the GAC did send, the first one – as related by Sgt. Kanipe - lacked any sense of urgency, while it is even questionable whether or not the second message actually originated with GAC or was sent by Cooke on his own initiative. Given the appearance and wording of the note it seems to have been written in haste and perhaps even panic.

After considering the timeline, and trooper dispositions, it is easy to see that GAC abandoned the rest of his command and not the other way around, as has been often claimed.

The volley gunfire heard at 1625, most likely, signaled the start of GAC's fight with the Sioux and the volleys heard at 1710 effectively signaled the end of the fight. That is, GAC's fight had lasted 45 minutes and was over before any possible effective support could arrive.

Any attempt by either Reno or Benteen would not have made a difference. If either had gone on alone, they would have suffered the same fate. Once they were combined with the extra troopers from B company and the rest of the pack train escort, time had already runout for Custer and his five companies.

Who won?

Most will claim that the united tribes won the battle, but this is open to question. Traditionally, the combatant that retains possession of the field of battle is the victor, and in this case, that would be the commands of Reno and Benteen. The tribes simply moved on, as they always did.

By their success in annihilating Custer's and five of the twelve regimental companies, the tribes created an even stronger incentive for the Army to continue and even escalate their desire to subjugate the tribes in any manner possible. The war against the Sioux and Cheyenne, as well as other tribes of the plains and Rocky Mountains, would go on another fourteen years.

1.4 Custer's Last Battle

Coda: The 400-Year War

The date, 12 October 1492, the day Columbus first made landfall, is as good as any date for the beginning of the occupation of the western hemisphere by Europeans. That is, it dates the start of the 400-year conflict between Europeans and the indigenous people of the western hemisphere.

At first, Columbus thought he had made it to the Indies and therefore named the natives Indios, the Spanish name for Indians. After a short *friendly* period, relations deteriorated to open conflict and the 400-year war was on!

The conflict that started in 1492, on the Island of San Salvador, can be said to have lasted until 1890, which for all practical purposes is 400 years of conflict. The date 1890 seems appropriate since that was the year that the US Army fought at Wounded Knee, Montana its – officially – last battle against the native peoples of North America.

Appendix: Custer's Orders from General Terry

Headquarters of the Department of Dakota (In the Field)
Camp at Mouth of Rosebud River, Montana Territory June 22nd, 1876
Lieutenant-Colonel Custer,
7th Calvary

Colonel: The Brigadier-General Commanding directs that, as soon as your regiment can be made ready for the march, you will proceed up the Rosebud in pursuit of the Indians whose trail was discovered by Major Reno a few days since. It is, impossible to give you any definite instructions in regard to this movement and were it not impossible to do so the Department Commander places too much confidence in your zeal, energy, and ability to wish to impose upon your precise orders which might hamper your action when nearly in contact with the enemy. He will, however, indicate to you his own views of what your action should be, and he desires that you should conform to them unless you shall see sufficient reason for departing from them. He thinks that you should proceed up the Rosebud until you ascertain definitely the direction in which the trail above spoken of leads. Should it be found (as it appears almost certain that it will be found) to turn towards the Little Bighorn, he thinks that you should still proceed southward, perhaps as far as the headwaters of the Tongue, and then turn toward the Little Horn, feeling constantly, however, to your left, so as to preclude the escape of the Indians passing around your left flank.

The column of Colonel Gibbon is now in motion for the mouth of the Big Horn. As soon as it reaches that point will cross the Yellowstone and move up at least as far as the forks of the Big and Little Horns. Of course, its future movements must be controlled by circumstances as they arise, but it is hoped that the Indians, if upon the Little Horn, may be so nearly enclosed by the two columns that their escape will be impossible. The Department Commander desires that on your way up the Rosebud you should thoroughly examine the upper part of Tullock's Creek, and that you should endeavor to send a scout through to Colonel Gibbon's command.

The supply-steamer will be pushed up the Big Horn as far as the forks of the river is found to be navigable for that distance, and the Department Commander, who will accompany the column of Colonel Gibbon, desires you to report to him there not later than the expiration of the time for which your troops are rationed, unless in the mean time you receive further orders.

Very respectfully, Your obedient servant,
E. W. Smith, Captain, 18th Infantry A. A. J. G.

1.4 Custer's Last Battle

Attachments

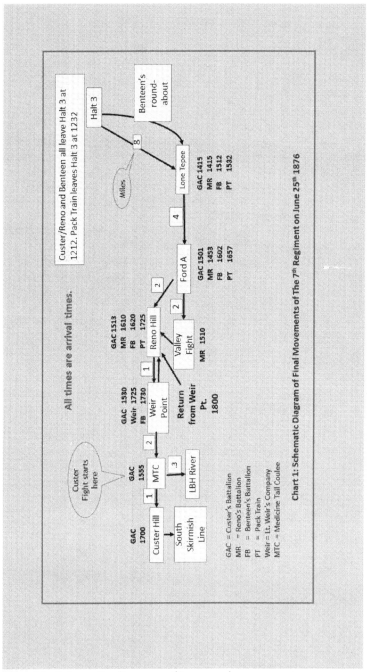

Chart 1: Schematic diagram of troopers' movements.

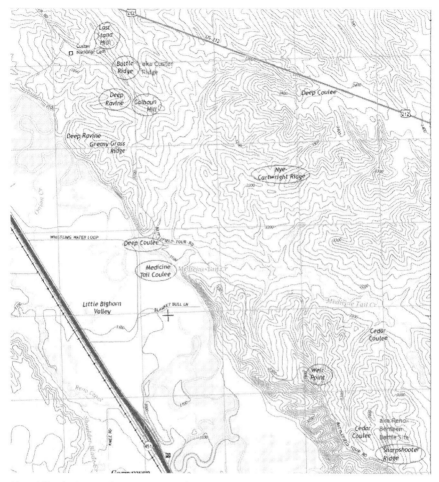

Map-1 Battle Area: The Custer battle field and the Reno-Benteen Battle field.[77]

---

[77] USGS Crow Agency 2014. NSN. 7643016376206 NGA REF NO. USGS X24K10849

1.4 Custer's Last Battle

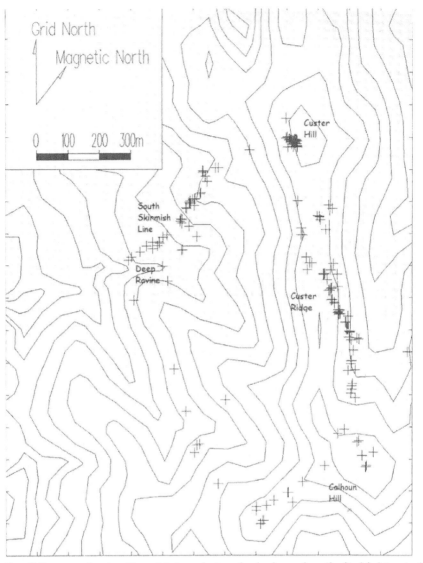

Map-2 Grave-marker locations: Markers clusters clearly show where the final fighting took place. Most are in the areas of Custer Ridge, Custer Hill, and South Skirmish Line.[78]

---

[78] R. A. Fox, *Archaeology, History, and Custer's Last Battle* (Norman, Univ. of Oklahoma Press,1993), Figure 6-8.

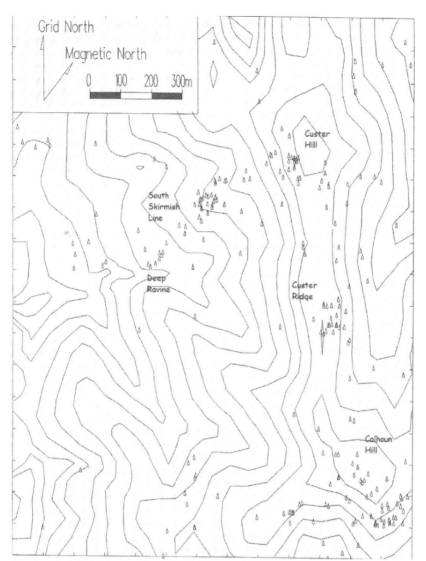

Map-3 Indian bullet locations: Bullet clusters clearly show concentrations of fire at the labeled locations.[79]

---

[79] R. A. Fox, *Archaeology, History, and Custer's Last Battle* (Norman, Univ. of Oklahoma Press,1993), Figure 6-9.

1.4 Custer's Last Battle

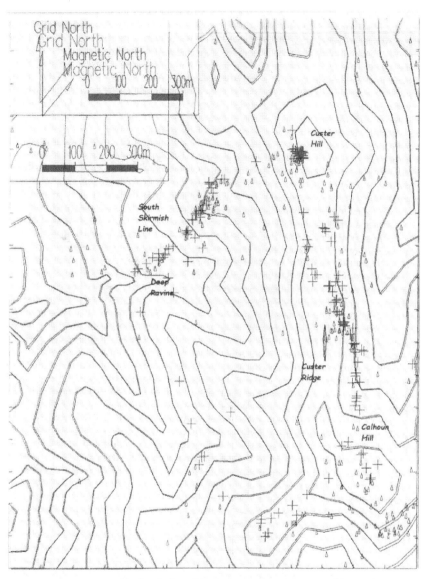

Map-4 Grave Markers and Indian Bullets: This is an overlay of Map-2 and Map-3.[80]

---

[80] R. A. Fox, Archaeology, History, and *Custer's Last Battle* (Norman, Univ. of Oklahoma Press,1993), Composite Fig 6-8 and 6-9.

1.5 The Second Thirty Years War: 1914 - 1945

Reconsidering the World Wars of the 20th Century

Introduction

Almost exactly 300 years after the *First Thirty Years War*, Europe was again plunged into a horrific conflict but this time the human and property cost reached a point of being unmeasurable and unimaginable.

Although this war was fought in the 20th century, the origins can be found in the aftermath of the First thirty years war. Following the end of this war in 1648, Europe, especially the German speaking principalities of central and eastern Europe, started a period of recovery, which lasted for several generations and well into the 18th century.

These devastated areas of central Europe were still not fully recovered by the 1740s, when Frederick (the Great) was anointed King of Prussia. Prussia lying far to the east, did not suffer the same fate as most other German speaking principalities did in that last major religious war in Europe and, consequently, was prosperous and had the restless energy required for a nation looking to extend its borders.

This relative strength and his neighbor's relative weakness, gave Frederick the opportunity to begin a program of subjugation and annexation at the expense of his neighbors to the west, and this he did, through extended campaigning that essentially lasted for his entire reign of 47 years!

Without going into details, Frederick's momentum, with the exception of a brief period during Napoleon's military adventures through central and eastern Europe, continued into the 19th century and eventually, in 1870-71, led to the establishment, as a result of France's defeat and humiliation in the Franco-Prussian War, of the German Second Reich with the coronation of Wilhelm the First as Kaiser.[81]

---

[81] The First Reich was the thousand-year Holy Roman Empire which effectively began with Charlemagne in 800 and ended in 1806.

1.5 The Second Thirty Years War: 1914 - 1945

Not only did France suffer military humiliation but also lost two provinces – Alsace and Lorraine. This humiliating loss of French national pride was destined to simmer for a generation and more. What no one knew, at that time, was that the Franco-Prussian War was destined to be the last traditional war in Europe. That is, where after some limited fighting that usually lasted only a few months, the victor would receive compensation of either money or/and territory, then everyone would go home until the next time.[82]

Although both World Wars I and II were global affairs, in the interest of brevity, I have mainly focused, in both cases, on the conflict in western Europe. In any case, since thousands of books and essays have been written about these wars, it is not necessary to go into great details, it suffices to mainly discuss only the broader picture.

---

[82] Some might think that the Boer War was the last traditional European war but this war, fought from 1899 to 1902, was more closely a preview of what the next wars would be like. For the first time, smokeless powdered weapons were used in a large conflict as well as modern artillery using cordite and other high explosives. This war also added the name *concentration camp* to the military lexicon.

Preparing for the Storm

By the early 20th century, there was an interesting peculiarity in Europe at that time. This was the proliferation of the children and grandchildren of Queen Victoria of England. For example, by 1910, following the death of Edward the Eighth – Victoria's eldest son – three of Victoria's grandsons were reigning monarchs in Europe. George V in England, Wilhelm II in Germany, and Nicholas II was Czar in Russia.

It seems that prior to 1900, the future Edward VIII and Wilhelm II, uncle and nephew, got along fairly well. Both were strongly inclined to nautical interests and both were strong supporters of their respective navies. The problems began when Wilhelm began a ship building program that the English thought threatened what the English considered to be their *Divine Right* to be masters of the world's oceans.

The Kaiser, an admirer of the British Navy, wished to have some level of naval parity with England, while the English were adamantly opposed to any country reaching even slight parity. This prompted a naval ship building race that lasted approximately from 1898 to 1912, by which time both countries had stretched their finances to the limit.

Previously, in 1894, prior to this naval race, France, seeking to surround Germany and find allies, joined with Russia in an alliance of mutual aid against any enemy that might attack the other. Although, unnamed in the alliance, the obvious *enemy* was, of course, Germany.

Later, in the early 1900s, other important alliances were concluded, most notably were the *Entente Cordial*, which was an agreement, between France and England (1904), and the other was the *Anglo-Russian Entente* between England and Russian (1907).

The Entente Cordial officially dealt mostly with colonial matters, but it also had the effect of establishing stronger ties between these two countries who had been at odds with each other for literally hundreds of years. Although not a true mutual aid alliance, it more or less came down to that in 1914. Likewise, the Anglo-Russian arrangement was officially a colonial agreement but did improve relations between these two countries whose monarchs were cousins.

It should be noted that throughout the years before the start of World War I, the only ally Germany had was the polyglot Austro-Hungarian Empire, which because of the loosely held allegiances of its ethnically diverse

1.5 The Second Thirty Years War: 1914 - 1945

provinces, was always in a state of unrest, or even open conflict, somewhere within its vast holdings.[83]

The Austro-Hungarian Empire had at least ten major languages along with numerous minor languages and dialects, which essentially meant that communication across the Empire was difficult and it meant that since each of these linguistically separate ethnic groups did not assimilate into the mainstream Austria or into mainstream Hungary, there was constant unrest due to cultural conflicts and incompatibilities.

This then, in a nutshell, illustrates some of the goings on between 1871 and 1914. There were, of course, numerous other international affairs and incidents with various degrees of importance but the essential point is that tension within Europe continued to grow until reaching the breaking point on the 28th of June, 1914 with the well-known assassination of Archduke Franz Ferdinand and his wife while on a visit to Sarajevo.

Following these assassinations, the Austro-Hungarian government first seeks the help of Germany in a war against Serbia, not receiving a definite answer, they then drew up an ultimatum for the Serbians, which contained impossible conditions that Serbia could not and would not agree to.

This ultimatum essentially guaranteed war, and on July 28, one month after the assassinations, Austria-Hungary declares war on Serbia and Russia orders general mobilization.

---

[83] With a secret agreement signed on August 2, 1914, Turkey also joined with Germany and Austria-Hungary alliance that was generally referred to as the Central Powers.

General Mobilization

On August 1st, Germany declared war on Russia and ordered general mobilization, and that same day, France ordered general mobilization but without a declaration of war. Two days later, August 3rd, Germany hastily declares war on France and committed itself to an ill-advised two-front war, in an act that shows how reason had given way to irrational militarism.[84]

The very next day, August 4th, Germany violates Belgium neutrality and pours troops over the border. This action immediately prompts England, because of a treaty agreement that *guaranteed* Belgium neutrality, England declares war on Germany.

Thus, began a war that all participants expected to be a short and traditional war but due to modern technology, the scope of the conflict, and other factors that are difficult to define, the war in the west, within just over a month, managed to reach a tactical stalemate that caused both the Allies (France and England) and Germany to stabilize the western front and begin what became known as *trench warfare*.

Instead of the traditionally short war like that of 1870 where it was over in a few months and the result was the exchange of two French provinces, this one would last just over 51 months, and would change the world forever, especially the world of the West.

---

[84] It should be noted, that also during this first week of August, various other countries, including the US declared their neutrality.

1.5 The Second Thirty Years War: 1914 - 1945

Stalemate: 1914 - 1916

As mentioned above, on August 4th, German troops violated Belgium neutrality by crossing over the border and the war on the western front began, while, in the east, things were somewhat slower getting started. This was the German plan to sweep into northern France and encircle Paris from the north and west[85]

Following the initial contact between the German and French armies, there followed about six weeks of mobile warfare, where at first, the French were driven back to about 40 miles from Paris before they were able to stop the Germans at the *First Battle of the Marne*. This crucial battle prompted a general withdrawal of the Germans that stopped with both armies were stretched from the English Channel in the north to the frontiers of Switzerland in the south and both sides began to dig in.

All this happened because the German plan to encircle Paris (Schlieffen Plan) and force an armistice failed, and it failed because the Belgium army proved to be a tougher nut to crack than the Germans had counted on. Instead of running over this small country, the Germans were held up by a series of forts that refused to surrender and had to be bombarded for days before they would surrender.

Meanwhile, on the eastern front, another unexpected series of events occurred. The Russians mobilized much sooner than the Germans expected and were able to advance well into Prussia before being out maneuvered and soundly defeated at the Battle of Tannenberg (August 1914).

The failure of the Schlieffen Plan and the early mobilization of the Russian armies meant that Germany's hope of quickly finishing off the French before the Russians were fully mobilized failed, and with this failure, the war was destined to be a long one.

Neither side had been able to overrun the other and mobile warfare turned into static defensive warfare of almost impregnable sets of trenches. Each side built defensive positions in depth such that each had multiple rows of trenches extending more than a mile behind the first line of trenches.

---

[85]This was the Schlieffen Plan which required quick passage through Belgium. However, Belgium proved to be a tougher nut than Germany expected. The siege of the Liege fortress ring of twelve forts delayed the German advance for about two weeks and put their plan hopelessly behind schedule. They could not be bypassed because the Germans need the railroad hub in Liege to supply their armies as they advanced into France.

While all this was going on in Europe, there were other events taking place on other fronts, but the main show was always the western front and without a resolution there the war would continue indefinitely.

Two Battles

Although, for the entire duration of this war, there was always fighting somewhere, these two battles provide a clear illustration of the profligate waste of human life and national treasure that exemplifies the First World War, especially the war on the western front.

Verdun: February 1916 – December 1916

This battle, between the Germans and the French, was the longest and one of the bloodiest of the war. The losses on both sides were almost unbelievable. Although the exact number of casualties is not known, the estimates are, at least, 400,000 French casualties with 140,000 killed and 379,000 German casualties with 163,000 killed.

The net result of all this slaughter was negligible and the Verdun front was much the same as it was before.

Somme July 1916 – November 1916

On July 1, 1916, the French and British launched a joint attack on German positions in the area of the Somme. Although, this battle was somewhat shorter that the Verdun battle, it was larger in number of participants and in number of casualties. In fact, it was the largest and bloodiest of the war.

On the first day, the British suffered something like 57,000 casualties with about 20,000 killed. This was without doubt the greatest single day loss by any of the belligerents during the war and the largest ever for the British Empire.

More than three million soldiers from both sides participated in this battle and, by the time it was over, it is estimated, that the Germans had suffered as many as 500,000 casualties, while the French and the British together suffered about 600,000 casualties. Again, after all that slaughter, the front remained essentially the same.

The statistics for these two battles are indicators of the inability of commanders on either side to come up with any method of breaking the stagnation and defensive capabilities of their opponents. This was true for

1.5 The Second Thirty Years War: 1914 - 1945

almost the entire war and it wasn't until the spring of 1918 that a method of penetrating these seemingly impenetrable trench systems was finally developed.

The Turn of the Tide: 1917 - 1918

By the third year, 1917, the major European belligerents were exhausted, almost bled dry, and had little to show for all the waste of national treasure, the most precious being the lives of the young men, who had by the end of the third-year suffered casualties into the millions.

This same year saw two occurrences that changed everything, in the sense that perhaps the war might end after all. The first event, which favored the Germans, was the February 1917 revolution in Russia that toppled the Romanov dynasty and within a few months took Russia out of the war and thus freed up about two million German soldiers for potential transfer to the western front.

The second event, which favored the Allies, was the April 6th declaration of war on Germany by the USA, this declaration would not only bring in fresh troops but provided a much need morale boost to the Allies. The only problem was that the American army, at that time, was totally unprepared for anything except the type of skirmishes taking place along the Mexican border that had been ongoing since 1910 and were to last into 1919.

However, by June of 1917, the US was somehow able to scrape together enough troops for a show of force and commitment to the Allies with the arrival of the first US troops in Europe, ever. These first token troops were the beginning of a mass influx of US troops that poured into France at an ever-increasing rate such that by May of 1918 over one million American soldiers had arrived.

In the meantime, over the winter of 1917-18, the Germans had transferred over a million men from the eastern front to bolster then commitment in the west and prepared for an *all or nothing* offensive in the spring.[86]

The German High Command realizing that with the American buildup would come disaster for the German army, they decided to put their final hopes into a massive offensive designed to split the French and British armies, while aiming at the capture of Paris.

---

[86]They should have transferred many more, but they miss-judged the situation in Russia by not realizing that Russian internal problems would prevent any renewal of the war against the Germans for years to come.

1.5 The Second Thirty Years War: 1914 - 1945

Consequently, on March 21st, the Germans launched their attack with more than 500,000 men on a 43-mile front. This was the first of a series of attacks that started out very successfully.

Using new tactics, this was the first great offensive of the war that actually made significant gains. The Germans had, for several months, been developing a new tactic for breaking the allied trench system that also introduced a new word into the military lexicon – the *Stormtrooper*.

Basically, this tactic used a fierce artillery barrage to break up the opponents barbed wire obstacles and drive the defending troops under ground, then, before the bombarded troops could recover, stormtroopers armed with light weight automatic firearms, hand grenades, and flamethrowers would quick follow-up behind the barrage.[87] The objective of these shock troops was not to totally subdue the first encountered lines of trenches, but to penetrate in depth and rely on follow-up troops to finish cleaning out the bypassed trenches.

At first, this tactic was very successful and the gains in the first few days were impressive, however, this offensive eventually lost momentum and after an unprecedented advance of as much as 40 miles the offensive came to a halt.

This slowdown and halt of the German offensive has been attributed to over extended supply lines, but many say the real reason was that after these undernourished troops penetrated behind the Allied front lines, they found huge quantities of food and wine such that the troops could not resist gorging themselves on this bounty and, simply, lost interest in pursuing the fleeing French and British.

In any case, the first attack was followed by a series of German assaults where each was less effective than the one before and by the end of July, the Germans had exhausted themselves and were forced back to the defensive. This was also the time when the impact of the infusion of fresh and eager US troops began to be felt.

Although, some French and British commanders were begging for US troops to be integrated within their existing units, the US commander-in-chief, General Pershing, refused to send his troops into combat piecemeal,

---

[87] This barrage was the largest of the war and in five hours, about 2.5 million artillery and mortar shells were fired at the Allies.

he demanded that the US troops fight as independent units, not as replacements for decimated French and English units.

By the summer of 1918, the US finally had enough trained troops to begin fielding their units at division and even corps level (2 to 3 divisions), and within a few months, the US frontline commitment had grown to several corps, which were organized as the US First Army and a second Army was in the process of being organized.

After the failure of the Germans spring offensive, the German army in the west was demoralized and greatly weakened by the loses sustained between March and July. On the other hand, this depleted condition of the German armies and the influx of the Americans gave the Allies the opportunity to start their own offensive.

This offensive, called the Hundred Day Offensive, was the last of the war and, by early November, the Allies had managed to push the Germans back to where they had started in March and beyond.

As it turned out, just when the US had reached a level of significance in the fighting, the fighting came to an end. In fact, the end came earlier than just about anyone had predicted when the German high command lost confidence and on November 9th, the Kaiser abdicated and fled to the neutral Netherlands.

This abdication precipitated quick action by the Germans and only two days later, the armistice was signed in the early hours of November 11, 1918 and by 11AM that day the guns fell silent. The fighting was over, but the long stretched out negotiations for a peace treaty were about to begin.

1.5 The Second Thirty Years War: 1914 - 1945

The Treaty of Versailles

The *Paris Peace Conference*, as the peace negotiations came to be known, started on January 18, 1919, and was to last about six months. Twenty-seven nations were represented by 70 delegates, but with only the Big Four (France, Britain, US, and Italy) really making a difference, and even then, it was the British and the French, especially the French, who were the main players.

From the beginning, the German delegation was treated poorly and vindictively by their French hosts. Hotel arrangements were poor, telephone lines tapped, and other forms of harassment were constantly used to keep the delegates uncomfortable and off balance. In any case, because the allies would not let them attend any negotiation sessions, they soon left Paris and returned to Germany.

French Issues
The French felt, and rightly so, that they had a special problem since they were the only major belligerent to share a common border with Germany. This made them especially anxious about a repeat performance and, consequently, their demands were more exacting than those of the other Allies.

For example, France wanted German territory west of the Rhine River, known as the Rhineland, set up as a buffer state between France and Germany. Failing in that effort, they did get an agreement that this territory should remain de-militarized and they would also be compensated with large amounts of German coal production.

Also, since most of the fighting on the western front was on French soil, they had a strong motive for the enactment of measures that would greatly weaken Germanies war making capability.

Side Comment About French goals: John Maynard Keynes, British economist and financial advisor to the British Peace delegation, had this to say:

"So far as possible, therefore, it was the policy of France to set the clock back and undo what, since 1870, the progress of Germany had accomplished. By loss of territory and other measures her population was to be curtailed; but chiefly the economic system, upon which she depended for her new strength, the vast fabric built upon iron, coal, and transport must be destroyed. If France could seize, even in part, what Germany was compelled to drop, the inequality of strength between the two rivals for European hegemony might be remedied for generations."[88]

Although, Germany did lose some territory, the German industrial capacity was hardly touched, it was still the results of the peace negotiations that were to do the lasting damage and in the long run manage to set up Europe for another fall.

British Issues

The British were not as hardline as the French. England itself had suffered little damage, except for the overwhelming tragic loss of almost a generation of young men.

After the casualties, it was the British economy that had taken such a beating that the country was deeply in debt and needed financial assistance. Before the war, Germany had been a major trading partner, and the British wished to reestablish this relationship now that the war was over and, of course, this required an economically healthy Germany.

As always, of major concern to the British was maintenance of their sea power and maintaining their colonial possessions.

American Issues

President Woodrow Wilson, a progressive democratic, had, before the November armistice, put together a list of fourteen points that he proposed as a foundational basis for the coming peace conference.

These fourteen points reflected Wilson's incurable idealism and were far from acceptable to the other members of the Big Four. For example, England, strongly objected to the clause #2 that called for the absolute freedom of the seas, while the French Prime Minister Clemenceau pointed out that the good God only needed ten points!

It is safe to say that his fourteen points were not overly popular with any of the Allies or the *Central Powers* (Germany, Austria-Hungary, Turkey).

---

[88] John Maynard Keynes, The Economic Consequences of the Peace (Harcourt Brace and Howe, 1920) p. 34

1.5 The Second Thirty Years War: 1914 - 1945

In any case, these fourteen points became something of a moot point, because the US eventually failed to ratify the peace treaty and even came to reject the *League of Nations* that had been the 14th point in Wilson's list! There were strong influences within the US that wanted the US to return to its old policy of isolationism and non-involvement in international, especially European, affairs.

German Issues

Needless to say, Germany had objections to the many of the more than 400 treaty clauses in the final peace document but the one that really stood out was #231 – known as the war guilt clause. This clause, essentially, and rather bluntly blamed the whole war on Germany.

This, of course, was a very hypocritical on the part of the Allies, since it is apparent to even the most casual student of the decades leading up to the war that the major belligerents, especially France, had been spoiling for a fight since the 1870s.

Anyway, in July 1919, after much discussion, the newly formed German government, known as the *Weimar Republic*, acted at the last minute and sent a delegation to Paris to sign – under protest – the treaty. Most likely, this only happened because the French held a pistol to Germany's head – so to speak – by announcing that they would invade western Germany, if they didn't![89]

Also, by this time, the summer of 1919, the myths and legends about the war were taking deep roots among many German veterans and, especially, those who had joined up with one of the numerous paramilitary groups that had formed since the armistice and demobilization.

There was a strong feeling within Germany that their armies had not been defeated in the field, but they were defeated by traitorous elements at home. The blame for the defeat was the *stab on the back* notion that named socialist, communists, and Jews for the betrayal of the German people, in general, and the German army, in particular.

---

[89] It should be noted, that even after the November Armistice, the Allies maintain their blockade of Germany, which meant that starvation in Germany still existed. It was not until January of 1919 that the blockade was partially lifted to allow food imports and it was not until July of 1919, after Germany signed the Peace Treaty, was the blockade completely lifted.

Japanese Issues

Although, Japan's role, compared with other powers, was relatively small, but they did reap a dividend that was the cause much trouble in the future. They managed to acquire all German mandates in the western Pacific Ocean that were north of the equator. This included the Marshall, the Carolinas, the Palau, and the Mariana Islands groups, all of which were to become scenes of bitter fighting in the 1940s.

Fallout from the Treaty

The war guilt clause, as previously mentioned, was a major problem in Germany and helped produce a bitterness against the Allies and especially France that was to simmer for the next 20 years.

Some historians site the order of mobilization as a sign of who the aggressors were, but this oversimplifies things too much, even though there may be a bit of truth in this sequence. By the summer of 1914, the temperament of the European powers had heated up and was just waiting for someone to pull the trigger. That someone turned out to be Gavrilo Princip. a radical Bosnian Serb, who, quite literally, pulled the trigger that started the war when he shot the Austrian Archduke and his wife.

But, perhaps, an even bigger and in the long run more important issue than the war guilt clause, was the demand for extortional reparation payments by Germany to various allies. The terms demanded payments equivalent to about 33 Billion US dollars, an enormous sum in those days.

This sum was far beyond the means of an economically impoverished Germany, and in order to meet these demands, Germany was forced to devalue their currency to the extent that hyper-inflation took hold and by 1923, Germany defaulted on payments, which prompted the French army to occupy the Ruhr industrial center in western Germany.

In addition to the reparation payments, the defeated nations had vast territories that greatly tempted the allied negotiators to divide up and re-allocate as newly formed independent countries or as annexations to existing countries on the winning side. These considerations seldom, if ever, gave serious or adequate consideration to ethnic or cultural issues and concerned themselves primarily with political and economic issues.

That is, the result was another example of how short sightedness seemed to govern most of the decisions made by the Peace Conference. For example, the newly formed Czechoslovakia, as the name indicates, lumped

1.5 The Second Thirty Years War: 1914 - 1945

together ethnic Czechs with ethnic Slovaks, as well as large portions of German speakers using territory that was formerly part of Austria-Hungary.

Other bad decisions included the British and French mandates in the middle east, which essentially guaranteed trouble in the future. In 1920, the British obtained a mandate for the parts of the southern Ottoman empire, which was given the generic name of Palestine, and the French received a more northern region that became the mandates of Syria and Lebanon.

These mandates were seen by the indigenous inhabitants as a betrayal of the promises made during the war in exchange for Arab help against the Turks.[90]

I needn't say much about this, because we are all too aware of the current situations that exist today (2018) in the Middle East.

Only one more territorial realignment will be mentioned, this is the re-creation of Poland out of spare parts of Germany, Austria-Hungary, and Russia, which made the mistake of incorporating within its borders a large number of ethnic Germans and ethnic Russians who were considered unwelcome guests by the majority of ethnic Poles. This combination, too, was to be the cause of much trouble in the future.

Generally speaking, the partitions and reallocations of territories were not accomplished wisely and in almost all cases the result was to only create more stress into the European states over the next two decades.

In the meantime, most of Europe and the US entered into the 1920s and enjoyed a decade of peace and a fragile prosperity.

---

[90] This is a reference to the Arab Revolt instigated by the British that made T. E. Lawrence famous. As *Lawrence of Arabia*.

Germany 1919 - 1933

Weimar Republic
Following the abdication of the Kaiser, the country was essentially without a government and, fearing a communist takeover, an anti-communist coalition quickly set about forming a new government and a new constitution. The first was accomplished within weeks, while the second was not completed until August of 1919.

However, even with a new government, the political situation in Germany was unsettled during the months between the armistice and the establishment and acceptance of the Weimar constitution in August 1919. But even with the new constitution, the country was unsettled by a proliferation of political parties and para-military organizations that on occasion resorted to violence to make their points.

This political chaos together with the economic hardships caused by the war and the reparation payments made it difficult for the government to maintain control.

Probably because of the German sense of order, somehow the new government did manage to hold together even through the hyperinflation of 1923 and by 1924 things in Germany were stabilized enough for the country to have regained some semblance of normalcy.

However, beneath the surface there was still considerable discontent over the loss of the war and the harsh demands of the Versailles treaty. As mentioned above, many, if not most, Germans felt that their armies had not been defeated in battle, but by treasonable action on the home front. It was the *stab in the back* notion that continued to be a prominent political issue throughout the 20s.

Even with this background discontent, between 1924 and 1929, the Weimar Republic, as the new government came to be known, enjoyed popular support and the roaring 20s bought time for Germany to settle into its new post-war situation.

Then came the Great Depression and the economies of the developed countries started to take on a change for the worse. As unemployment increased, civil unrest in Germany increased and this unrest gave a small political entity called the National Workers Party the chance it had been waiting for.

1.5 The Second Thirty Years War: 1914 - 1945

National Socialism on the Rise

It Seems that in July of 1919, the army in Munich sent a corporal to infiltrate a small political party called *The German Workers' Party*, and by September he succeeded in being allowed to attend one of their closed meetings.

It was at this meeting that this corporal became noticed when he got into an argument with one of the members and, apparently, he spoke so well that he was invited to join up. So, after just one meeting with this nascent organization, the young corporal, Adolf Hitler, was accepted as a member of the party.

After that Hitler's life began to change and within about a year he managed to become the Chief of Propaganda for the party that, since he joined, had grown from less than one hundred members attending a meeting to more than 2000 attending. Clearly, Hitler knew the temper of the German people and how to exploit that knowledge.

Throughout the 1920s, the party did not really amount to much, but the depression changed their future and they were soon on the rise to becoming a major player in German politics.

The economic crisis of the depression hit Germany in 1930 when US banks cut off their credit lines with Germany and by July of that year, a moratorium stopped the reparation payments, and by 1932, as the financial crisis deepened, most reparation payments were simply canceled.

By this time, both the Communist Party and the Nazi Party were gaining rapidly in popularity and the race was on between these two parties for control of Germany

World War II Starts in Asia: 1931

The Manchurian Incident

The Japanese, for economic reasons, had had their eye on the Chinese province of Manchuria for some time, but had restrained from any forcible act against the local Manchurian government.

This started to change in 1931, when the new Chinese government[91] announced that existing treaties with Japan were invalid. This meant that they wanted the Japanese troops, who had been *protecting* a railroad in Manchuria since about 1906, out of Manchuria.[92]

The response by the Japanese army in Manchuria was to stage an incident such that they could claim that the Chinese were the aggressors. So, on September 18, 1931, they set off a bomb that apparently only damaged about 8 feet of a single rail of the Japanese protected railroad![93]

The very next day, about 500 Japanese soldiers attacked a local Chinese garrison of about 7000. Although greatly outnumbered by the Chinese, the experienced Japanese troops easily defeated the disorganized and ill-equipped Chinese.

After this incident, there followed much international discussion, led by the ineffective League of Nations, with very little in action, such that this incident went unpunished and became the start of the Second World War in the Pacific where open hostilities between China and Japan was to last for another fourteen years!

---

[91] This was the Nationalist Chinese government under Chiang Kai-shek.

92 The Japanese army had been in Manchurian for several decades on the pretense of guarding the South Manchurian Railway.

[93] This incident was only the latest of a series that continually increased the tensions between the Japanese and the Newly formed Chinese Nationalist government.

1.5 The Second Thirty Years War: 1914 - 1945

The Third Reich: 1933 - 1939

Hitler Becomes Chancellor

By the summer of 1932, both the depression and the fear of a communist takeover had boosted the Nazi Party and in the summer of 1932, they received 37% of the popular vote for Reichstag (parliament) membership. However, because of the voting split between all of the parties, it was not possible to form a majority coalition, which meant that normal governing was not possible within the Weimar system.

This was the Nazi Party's high-water mark of the popular vote, by November 1932 when another election was called by the then Chancellor, Franz von Papen, in the hope of getting a workable coalition, the Nazi's support dropped to about 30%.

Following the November election there was still no resolution to the lack of a coalition and over the next two months behind the scene negotiations were going on with Franz von Papen and others trying to persuade President Hindenburg that since the Nazi Party still receive the largest block of votes in November, that Hitler should be appointed chancellor.

As vice-chancellor, Papen felt that with the help of Hindenburg, Hitler could be controlled. This might have seemed reasonable since the position of chancellor, at that time, was more a figurehead position rather than a power position. Hindenburg was finally convinced, or at least agreed, and Hitler was appointed chancellor on January 30, 1933.

Hitler almost immediately set about changing, by any means available, the position of chancellor into a power position. And, the means he chose were a clear indication of what to expect from Hitler in the future when, less than a month after his appointment, Hitler and his henchmen arranged to start a fire at the Reichstag and place blame on the communists. This prompted Hindenburg to issue the *Reichstag Fire Decree*, which was the first of many decrees to come that began the curtailment of German liberties.

Hitler Becomes Dictator

The Reichstag Fire Decree was only the beginning, and in March of 1933, Hitler was able to get the so-called *Enabling Act* passed by 2/3 majority of the Reichstag. This act essentially gave Hitler and his Nazi dominated cabinet virtual dictatorial powers for a period of four years and even allowed ignoring the constitution, in certain cases.

Over the next year, Hitler continued in various ways to consolidate and increase his power and the final piece that he needed came his way in August of 1934 when on the death of President Hindenburg, Hitler appointed himself president. Hitler's internal power-grab was now complete, and as virtual dictator, he was now able to pursue other agendas.

Rearmament and Land Grabs
By 1938, Hitler was absolute ruler of Germany and, after five years as Chancellor and four years as President, Hitler, in violation of the Treaty of Versailles, was well on the way to having rebuilt the German armed forces such that he felt strong enough to start the execution of his territorial agendas.

March of this year (1938) Hitler, partly by force of intimidation and partly voluntary, he made his first land grab by the annexation his native country, Austria, into the Third Reich.

A year later, in March 1939, although rearmament was still not complete, he felt that the time was again right to flex this military muscle power with the annexation of parts of Czechoslovakia, which you will recall from above that was a country put together in 1919 from spare parts of the Austrian-Hungarian empire and contained a large German speaking population who resided primarily in border regions known collectively as the Sudetenland.

Hitler simply moved troops across the common border and occupied those parts of Czechoslovakia that he wanted. To this action of aggression, the former allied powers simply voiced their objections and did nothing!

Again, the western powers did essentially nothing but complain a little and after talking things over with Hitler some were even convinced that he had made his last territorial demands and that there would be no more such land grabs. The western powers seemed content with Hitler's promises and so they chose to follow the path of appeasement and accommodation.[94]

OF course, after Austria and Czechoslovakia, Hitler was not even close to being territorially satisfied and he turned to the east toward his next victim.

---

[94] Appeasement and accommodation was made official on September 30, 1938, with the signing by France, Great Britain, Germany, and Italy of the so-called *Munich Agreement*. The Czech government was not invited to the conference that dismember their country.

1.5 The Second Thirty Years War: 1914 - 1945

The months following the March invasion of Czechoslovakia, were spent both pretending to be Poland's friend and at the same time making demands on Polish territory and the Free city of Danzig. Also, during this time, England, making a rare firm stand, stated that they would protect the city of Danzig, on behalf of Poland, and thereby committed themselves in case of war between Germany and Poland.

But, the big surprise of 1939, was the *German-Soviet Non-Aggression Pact*[95] that was made public 0n August 23. There was both shock and suspicion with this announcement, there was shock because these two countries were politically at odds and there was suspicion about the true meaning of this pact.

---

[95] Also known as the Molotov–Ribbentrop Pact.

Start of Aggressive War: 1939 - 1945

Blitzkrieg Tested on Poland

On September 1, less than two weeks after the announcement of the non-aggression pact, the suspicions about the pact were confirmed, when based on a phony accusation, German troops crossed the border into Poland and the Second World War in Europe began.

Within three days, in support of Poland, both the British and the French declared war on Germany, however, except for a few scattered and unimportant acts, both remain impotently on the sidelines as Germans troop overwhelm the Poles in only five weeks.

The hidden agenda of the non-aggression pact became apparent when, only two weeks into the fighting, the Soviets also invade Poland from the east and in a matter of days, moved west toward a pre-arranged line of demarcation that was to divide Poland between Germany and the USSR.

After the fall of Poland, a strange thing happened. This strange thing was that, although Germany, France and Great Britain were in a state of war, almost nothing happened for the next seven or so months! It was the calm before the storm.

Hitler Moves North

Finally, on April 9, 1940, the German, surprised the world again, when they suddenly invaded Norway. There was no way that Norway could resist this invasion. Most of the fighting was between the Germans and British, who did not like the idea of Germany controlling the eastern North Sea.

This relatively easy subjugation of Norway, had both tactical and strategic consequences for Germany. Tactically, they could threaten England and Scotland from a different direction and, strategically, this move was to protect the sea routes for the shipments of iron ore and other raw materials from the northern parts of neutral Sweden that were on their way to Germany.

Blitzkrieg in the West

While the Germans and the British were still picking away at each other in Norway, the real struggle for Europe began on May 10, when Germany invaded Belgium, France, Luxembourg, and the Netherlands with overwhelming force and in a manner not expected.

1.5 The Second Thirty Years War: 1914 - 1945

The Allies (France and England) were still thinking back to 1914 and the Schlieffen Plan, which called for the German armies to attempt an encirclement of Paris from the north and west. And, since the Germans were, again appeared to be coming through Belgium, they supposed that it was business as usual and, just as they did in 1914, rushed most of their mobile troops to the French-Belgium frontier.

They were partially correct, the Germans were coming that way, but that was only a feint, they were also coming in a way that was totally unexpected and was thought by the obsolete senior allied commanders to be both impassable and impossible.

This unexpected route was the Ardennes Forest area that lay south of the Belgium-French frontier and north of France's massive and infamous Maginot Line fortifications. This mountainous area, having only narrow meandering roads, was protected by only a few weak French divisions, but this is where the bulk of the German armored and motorized divisions struck.

Contrary to standard military thought, these German mechanized and armored forces were able to penetrate the Ardennes with relative ease and within two weeks had completely cut off the French and English forces that had advanced to the Belgium frontier.

The Allies soon found themselves surrounded and backed up to the English Channel. Having no other choice except surrender, on May 27, the British, along with some French and Belgium soldiers, began to evacuate from the channel port of Dunkirk in a remarkable operation, aided by German unexplained inactivity. Eventually, they managed to rescue over three hundred thousand troops. Of course, in true British style, they managed to convince most of the world that this evacuation was actually a victory.

The real situation was a disaster for the Allies and instead of the stalemate and years of trench warfare, the French and English forces found themselves soundly beaten in less than two months!
Paris was occupied on June 14th and on June 22nd the French surrendered in the same rail car that had been used by the French in 1918 for the signing of the November 1918 armistice and with that French humiliation, for the second time in less than a century, was essentially complete – after the signing, the German destroyed the rail car and the 1918 armistice memorial site where it had been kept.

Once again, a false calm came over most of Europe. To be sure, there was still major fighting going on in North Africa and other places, but for almost another year Germany was able to consolidate its current gains and plan for the next step.

Taking on the Colossus
In spite of the legendary curse that proclaimed that a violation of the tomb of Tamerlane the Great would bring war and disaster, on June 20, 1941, the Soviets opened his tomb and removed the remains.

Two days later, the Germans, who had massed about three million solders on the border, launched an undeclared invasion in to the Soviet Union.

The die was cast, and for the Germans, it was a race against the time and the coming of the Russian winter. They had to either subdue their opponent or, at least, achieve a position where they could safely survive the winter while maintaining an offensive advantage.[96]

Initially, the most massive invasion in history went well for the Germans and badly for the Soviets. In the first phase of the German offensive, the Soviets were totally outclassed militarily and suffered greatly from lack of organization and suffered severe casualties.

It has been estimated that the Soviets had more casualties in the first two weeks of this battle than the US suffered throughout the entire war! The Germans offensive was at high tide throughout the summer of 1941 and into the autumn, such that by November they had advanced almost one thousand miles and were threatening Moscow.

But then, something happened, it turned cold, then it turned very cold and in early December, the German fighting machine ground to a halt just a few miles from the Soviet Capitol.

Turn of the Tide
Although almost no one realized it, it was the beginning of end for the Germans, but like so many turning points, this one, being unrecognized as a turning point, was followed by to a long and bitter fight to the finish.

---

[96] The line that had been in the planning has been called the *Archangel-Astrakhan Line* since the line stretched from Archangel on the northern White Sea south to Astrakhan on the Caspian Sea.

Consequently, over the next three plus years, the fighting between the Colossus of the East and Germanic Hordes would prolong this greatest and most horrific of all battles until the German armies were driven back to Berlin and, essentially, the entire country was overrun by foreign troops.

The youth of both nations bled in the millions as the human cost continued to rise to unimaginable levels. The tenacity of both sides was tested to the known limits of human endurance and beyond where new levels of endurance were set.

Closing the Ring
In the west, the western Allies, mainly the US and the British, were not completely idle. Although both, especially the US, were deeply involved with the war in Asia, both the British and the US had committed to the defeat of Hitler first and, as a consequence, allocated most of their resources to this purpose.

By November 1942, after the British had been fighting the Germans and Italians in North Africa for almost two years, the US was finally able to become part of the land fighting, with the landing of several divisions in northwest Africa. This action was designed to put the German army in north Africa into a two-front situation and hasten the defeat of what was commonly called the Africa Corps.

Partly, because of the inexperienced US troops and, partly because of the abilities of the seasoned Africa Corps troops, this defeat of the German and Italian forces took much longer than anticipated and had the longer effect of getting the US involved in the Mediterranean Sea area to the extent that they were unable to get out until the end of the war.[97]

However, the African mis-adventure did teach the US a lot about modern warfare and this knowledge would was to prove invaluable in the coming struggle in western Europe.

In any case, the much-touted invasion of western Europe began on June 6, 1944, and the western Allies were, finally, able to put enough pressure on German resources such that German strength had to be lessened in the

---

[97] By July of 1943 the US was fighting in Sicily and in September they were, along with the British, on the European mainland and moving, slowly, up the Italian boot.

East. Of course, by this time, after fighting the Germans almost alone for three years, the Soviets had the Germans in full retreat and had essentially pushed the Germans out of all Soviet territory and were advancing into Poland.[98]

In the West, the allied invasion of the Normandy coast got off to a slow start because the British were not able to capture the German stronghold around the French city of Caen. The British commander, Marshal Montgomery, who was both arrogant in the extreme and sloth-like in his aggressiveness, had promised this city in a few days, but instead it took weeks before a general breakout from the invasion beachhead could be made.

When the breakout finally happened, the Allies were able to sweep across France in less than two months. Paris was liberated on August 25th, and the highly mechanized troops of the US and Britain, aided by a US invasion of southern France on August 15th, were able to liberate most of France by September 15th.

Then, as the allied armies were approaching the German frontiers, the German resistance stiffened and at the same time that the Allies began having trouble keeping their troops supplied – there were incidents where large mechanized units, quite literally, ran out of gas! The result was that little progress was made by the Allies from the middle of September through December 15th, and beyond.

Hitler's Gamble in the West

Then, December 16, the German's launched a massive counter-offensive that took the Allies completely by surprise. Allied intelligence services had not detected the massive German build-up and had underestimated the German capability of even launching an offensive of any kind, let alone one that involved almost a half million soldiers.

This attack came through the Ardennes Forest and had the very optimistic goal of reaching Antwerp that was nearly one hundred miles away. At first, the attack was very successful and by the 25th of December, the offensive

---

[98] In the West (US and England) the contribution of the Soviets to the defeat of Germany is almost always understated. It is estimated that more than 80 percent of German casualties occurred on the eastern front and this statistic, alone, speaks of significance of the Soviet contribution. But, it should also be noted, that the US provided crucial supplies to the Soviets without which they might not have survived.

1.5 The Second Thirty Years War: 1914 - 1945

had advanced to within a few miles of the River Meuse that lay about fifty miles from where the attack had started.

Then the attack faltered and due to supply problems, extremely cold weather, and American stubbornness the Bulge – as the salient came to be called – started to slowly shrink. The end of the offensive cam on January 25th when the front was almost completely restored to the positions held on December 15th.

As it turned out, actual casualties, for both sides, from all causes were almost even with each losing somewhere around 120,000 to 130,000 men. On the other hand, equipment loses were imbalanced with the Americans losing about 2,000 armored vehicles of all types while the Germans lost just over 500. However, the US could afford to lose 2000 armored vehicles whereas the Germans could ill afford to lose even 500 such vehicles.

Following the failure of the German offensive, the Allies were able to recovery all the territory lost, re-equip their armies, and prepare for their advance to the Rhine and the German homeland.

Spring Thaw in the West

However, because of stiff resistance and the very bad winter weather, it was not until March of 1945 that they were able to advance to the Rhine on a broad front and prepare to cross into Germany proper. It had taken many months to advance from the frontiers of eastern France to the Rhine and they were still hundreds of miles from Berlin, while at the same time, the Soviets were closing in on Berlin from the East.[99]

Finally, the Allies were able to cross the Rhine and from then on until the end of the fighting, they were able to make swift advances into the heart of Germany until they reached the Elbe River where their advance came to an end on meeting up with the Soviets on April 25th.[100]

At this point, the war against Germany was essentially over. Hitler committed suicide on April 30th, and a week later the Germans surrendered unconditionally to the western Allies and the Soviets.

---

[99] In September of 1944, the Allies were as close as 50 miles from the Rhine, but they were not able to cross in strength until March of 1945, a delay of six months.

[100] This was a pre-arranged line of demarcation.

The War in Asia

As discussed above the war in Asia started with Japanese aggression in Manchuria over an alleged railroad bombing. After this incident, no real action was taken against Japan such that Japan now felt that they were free to continue their plans to spread their aggression into the rest of China without fear of any meaningful reprisals from any of the western powers.

Consequentially, from 1932 on until 1945, there is active war between Japan and the Chinese that took the lives of as many as twenty-two million Chinese and about one million Japanese.

As is well known, the US did not become actively involved in the Asian war until after the December 7th, 1941 attack at Pearl Harbor, Hawaii, which did more than any other thing to motivate the US in its future war efforts. The Japanese had indeed awakened the sleeping industrial giant.

What followed was a long series of bloody battles where the Japanese fought with a ferocity not seen in the West and with a fatalism where surrender was not an option.[101] Besides the fanaticism of the Japanese military, this war was fought over most of the western half of the world's largest ocean, which meant that it was essential a naval war, where superiority at sea was essential for victory.

Although the war against Japan was to last more than three and a half years, by June 1942 and the *Battle of Midway*, there was no doubt that Japan had no chance of winning. This battle crippled Japan's naval offensive capability and turned Japan from the offensive to the defensive.[102] This was significant because, given the vastness of the Pacific Ocean, mobile air power in the form of aircraft carriers was the main strategic weapon.

By the early summer of 1945, the US was actively fighting in the Philippine Islands and on the Japanese home island of Okinawa. At Okinawa, the one hundred thousand defenders were fighting almost to the last man in a battle that foretold of what could be expected if it became necessary to invade Japan proper. In the Philippines, the US army was also engaged in fierce fighting that would still be going on at wars' end.

---

[101] In western Europe, Germans were eventually captured in the hundreds of thousands, while in Asia only a few thousand Japanese were captured.

[102] In that battle, the Japanese lost four of their best aircraft carriers but, of more importance, they also lost many of their best and most experienced pilots.

1.5 The Second Thirty Years War: 1914 - 1945

Based on the experience of these two and other battles, it was estimated that US forces could expect, at least, one million casualties before the Japanese could be defeated at home.

Even after many months of horrendous bombing with both conventional bombs and incendiary bombs, which caused incredible destruction and the deaths of several hundred thousand, the Japanese still did not give up and except for some rumors, there was no real indication that they would surrender.

This was one of the arguments that led the US President to decide to use the newly developed secret weapon as a motivation for surrender, and on August 6th, the first atom bomb to be used as a weapon was dropped on the Japanese city of Hiroshima, then three days later, a second atom bomb was dropped on the city of Nagasaki.

After these two bombs, the Japanese leadership was ready to quit, and the surrender followed quickly, and on August 15, 1945, the Japanese Emperor, Hirohito, endured the unendurable and announced to the world the surrender and the end of World War Two.

Was Use of the Atom Bombs Justified?

Although there appears to have been some government officials within Japan who were sympathetic or even actively pursuing a possible peace settlement, the powers at the top remain publicly adamant about a continuation of hostilities regardless of the cost and still had hopes or beliefs that the US would negotiate a settlement after the invasion of Japan proper because of the huge casualties that would be incurred.

Having stated that only unconditional surrender would be acceptable, the Allies put themselves in a box that they could not get out of and therefore had little or no recourse except to continue to pursue that end. With Germany out of the war, a quick end to war with Japan was, by any means, desperately desired by the war-weary Allies.

Consequently, when faced with the prospect that an invasion of Japan proper was estimated to cause as many as one million US casualties and with no real assurance that the Japanese were seriously considering surrender, the decision was made to use the only two atom bombs that were in existence at that time.[103]

In the end, after the dropping of the two atom bombs, the unconditional surrender demand was slightly eased by the decision to allow the Japanese Emperor to remain as emperor. This decision was met with some dispute from those who wanted the Emperor on trial as a war criminal, but the decision stood and from a political perspective it was a wise decision.

The physical and psychological effects of the bombs brought a quick end to the hostilities and this, in turn, kept the Soviet Union from grabbing more territory in Asia and assured that the US would be dominant in determining the future of Japan.

Finally, although this may seem cruel, given human nature and the length of the Cold War, it would have been inevitable that far more destructive nuclear bombs would have been used with far greater death and destruction than those that occurred at Hiroshima and Nagasaki. The horror of these weapons was made clear by their use, and it is this horror, which should never be forgotten. That is, this knowledge is the greatest deterrent to their future use.

---

[103] Earlier, in July 1945, a third bomb was exploded at a remote site in New Mexico as a necessary test of the atomic bomb concept.

1.5 The Second Thirty Years War: 1914 - 1945

Aftermath

The Germans and the Japanese Before WWII
Although, during the first half of the 20th century there were many differences between these two countries, there are a number of important similarities. Here is a list of some primary similarities.

1. Highly industrialized.
2. Socially disciplined with strong sense of social hierarchy.
3. Centuries old militarism.
4. Feeling of racial superiority over neighbors and certain cultures.
5. Love of pageantry or formal ceremonials.
6. Felt a need for territorial expansion.
7. Short on internal sources of certain strategic material – For example, petroleum
8. A tendency toward behavior bordering on fanaticism.
9. A feeling of lack of respect by others.
10. Strong work ethic.
11. Belief in a mystical destiny.

Of course, this isn't an all-inclusive list, but it is, perhaps, enough of a list to indicate how both countries somehow thought that they could successfully wage aggressive war against the rest of the industrialized world and win.

Most items on this list could apply, with various degrees of intensity, to many, if not most, industrialized countries and some not so industrialized. It is not just having or not having characteristics from the list as it is the degrees of intensity of these characteristics.

Anyway, like the so-called perfect storm, these listed elements and other considerations such as geographical location, recent history, and so on, all came together in the right intensity and combination to drive them to the self-destruction of aggressive warfare.

Changes: 1945 and Beyond
Just as these two countries had many common characteristics that led to war, after the war they found themselves in somewhat similar situations.

Both countries had suffered greatly from the loss of their young men in military service but unlike most other wars, the suffering of the homeland was also great. In Germany armies came from both east and west to scour the country side almost in its entirety, while at the same time Germany suffered great loss of life and property through aerial bombardment.

Although, Japan proper was not devastated by land armies, the aerial bombing was worse than that experienced by Germany. Besides the obvious horror of the two atomic bombs, Japan also suffered horrendously from the incendiary bombing of its largest cities where wooden construction was common, and the resulting firestorms killed in the hundreds of thousands.

After their defeat in 1945, instead of the strong reprisals applied at that time to the Central Powers, in 1919, the Allies, mostly the US, poured billions of dollars into rebuilding these countries, and many others who had been victims of either the Japanese or the Germans.

To be sure, reparation payments were demanded, by they were not at the level of those demanded after the First World War. Unlike the first war, these reparations were not designed to debilitate either Japan or Germany

As is well-known, Germany, besides losing large pieces of territory, was partitioned into four *Zones of Occupation* that, in reality, divided the country into two pieces; one in the west managed by the western Allies and one in the east managed by the Soviet Union as part of the eastern coalition that the Soviets had set up that essentially build a wall of Soviet satellite nations.[104]

In Japan the situation was far different. The occupation of Japan was an exclusive US affair and the senior Allied officer in the Pacific, General MacArthur, was installed as virtual dictator of the Japanese nation. He held this job for about five years, and by the end of that time, Japan had a new constitution and was well on its way to becoming the economic superpower of the far east.

The appointment of Douglas MacArthur as Supreme Allied Commander and *de facto* ruler of Japan, proved to be a wise decision. During his five years his benign and dignified rule won over the loyalty and admiration of the Japanese people, and firmly established Japan as a constitutional democracy.

---

[104] This is reference to the famous *Iron Curtain* that ideologically and physically divided western and eastern Europe after the war. This term – Iron Curtain – often mistakenly attributed to Winston Churchill, was actually first used in 1945 in the diary of the German Propaganda Minister Joseph Goebbels.

1.5 The Second Thirty Years War: 1914 - 1945

Because of the destruction and partitioning, building a new non-militaristic Germany took more time but it wasn't too many years before the economy of the western partitions was becoming an economic force in the world marketplace.

Coda

Obviously, the rebuilding of civilization after 1945 was long and complex such that it is only possible here to make only brief comments.

Today, there are a rapidly diminishing number of persons who remember the world of 1945, and an even fewer number alive today who were active participants. For the vast majority of those living today, especially the young, the Second Thirty Years War is almost ancient history. What they forget, or never knew, was how that thirty years changed the world in ways that are difficult to understand or explain adequately.

To this day, both Japan and Germany still have a large American military presence on their national soil and there doesn't seem to be any plans for their removal. They are no longer called occupation forces but are there as allies to help ensure the peace.

For more than 70 years, we have lived with the knowledge that humanity truly does have the capacity to destroy itself. It is, indeed, remarkable that, given the current proliferation of atomic weapons, that we as a species of impulse and sometimes great irrationality have refrained, since 1945, using these weapons against ourselves.

Part 2: Commentary on Contemporary Historical Writings

2.1 Miscellany of Preliminary Topics

Before getting onto the main topic of reconsidering contemporary historical writings, it seems appropriate to first offer a set of preliminary topics that are intended to provide some background and level setting for the subject matter that follows.

Some of these topics might not, at first, seem relevant to writing on historical subjects, but since writing on history is more than just historical events, well-written history includes elements of psychology, philosophy, sociology, and other cultural influences. With that in mind, I believe that these short topics are appropriate.

Judgments (hasty and otherwise)
Hasty judgments are often the result of the desire to make quick, easy decisions, and to avoid the extra effort of a more thoughtful choice. As a result, such decisions are often over-simplifications based on incorrect and/or incomplete information.

Judgments about complex issues are often decided from only a single *fact*, which is accepted as conclusive, while completely ignoring other pertinent issues. Basing a judgment on a single fact or belief is risky and sets a fragile foundation for belief that is easily toppled.

No doubt, it is much easier to base an opinion on a single piece of supposed evidence rather than consider a more complete and complex justification. However, this type of judgment, besides being fragile, often leads to hasty and invalid generalizations, which, in turn, can result in unwarranted stereotyping and the mistake of over simplification. Susceptibility to this type of error seems most prevalent when strong emotion is involved such as those inherent in political, cultural, or religious opinions.

To be sure, being able to decide or establishing a position with minimum effort is what makes slogans so popular and effective. Slogans are an attempt to simplify complexity and make it easier to adopt a certain opinion or decide upon a course of action. One is not required to know a lot about any issues or details; one just adopts and parrots the slogan.

Slogans do not even have to make any sense; they just have to be simple and easy to remember. In the USA, one of the most famous is the slogan from World War II; *Remember Pearl Harbor*! Recently, there was the political slogan; *Forward, not Backward*, which, although popular, was just an empty phrase.

Personalization is another vehicle for rash and unsubstantiated judgments. This is the case where an individual tends to over personalize the behavior of others based on their own personal choices.

For example, one might condemn a certain behavior because of an *I would never do that!* attitude. Such personalizing may seem harmless, except that it is often an over simplification tending toward negativity, which if left unchecked, can lead to unwarranted prejudices and condemnation.

Other common ways a person avoids thoughtful value judgments is through peer pressure or desire for group identification. This group identification seems one of the more popular pastimes (See Groupthink – page 150).

For example, over identification with sports teams or individual athletes is endemic and often borders on the fanatical (but then *fan* is just an abbreviation for *fanatic*). This, over identification with celebrities, is why advertisers use famous persons or persons of supposed authority in their commercials. Such inducements are artificial, but effective.

Of course, what has been mentioned here is only a small piece of how we make judgments and how personal opinions influence us. Unfortunately, opinions are often retained even after they are contradicted or falsified. *It is a fact, that a reassuring lie is often preferred over an inconvenient truth.*

Sufficient Evidence for Belief

What constitutes sound and sufficient evidence? Again, we fall back on that most human of answers; it depends. To be sure, this question is difficult or even impossible to answer completely. What seems sufficient to one person might well be far less than acceptable to another, and what comprises sound evidence for one person may be utter nonsense to another.

For example, many consider that the Judeo-Christian Bible is essentially one hundred percent true, while others see myths and allegory in much of the Bible, and still others believe that it is entirely apocryphal. This comment is not meant as a criticism, but as an example of how broadly interpretations and beliefs may vary, especially when highly emotional issues are considered.

Evidential sufficiency depends on subject matter and the world-view of the person making the judgment such that what is considered sufficient varies by both in form and kind. For example, evidence for the orbit of earth around the Sun is obviously different from legal evidence. The orbits of the earth and other planets around the sun has been unquestionably substantiated through unquestionable, although indirect and inferential, evidence.

On the other hand, what is considered valid legal evidence varies considerably by society. One is the work of nature and has essentially universal acceptance, while the other is the work of humans and like most human efforts are often somewhat arbitrary, subjective, or even capricious.[105]

When making decisions about such issues as morality, religion, and other emotional areas of human concern, the evidence for belief is always strongly influenced by the subjective. Additionally, we often base this subjective evidence on sparse information and mostly rely on personal intuition and disposition.

Intuition, depends on things such as prior experience, knowledge, observation, and ability to form inferentially sound judgments, while disposition relies on such things as existing prejudices, self-image, social factors, and so on.

It is quite common for someone to hold contradictory beliefs that are based on insufficient or inaccurate information. For example, in this country, gun control is often a volatile issue. Advocates both for and against gun control find it difficult to find any middle ground for compromise.

Those who strongly oppose gun control will be called Group A. Group A relies mainly on the Second Amendment to the US Constitution as providing the right to possess firearms and that this amendment does not specify any restrictions on type of firearms. On the other hand, there are those who strongly favor strict gun control, we will call this Group B. Group B seems to base their belief primarily on the substantial number of persons killed each year by firearms.

---

[105] However, it should be noted that in a 2014 survey 26% of those asked still thought that the Sun revolves around the earth! (NSF Survey 2014 National Science Board: Science and Engineering Indicators. 2014 Chapter 7;
http://www.nsf.gov/statistics/seind14/?org=NSF.)

2.1 Miscellany of Preliminary Topics

In addition to gun control, there is another strongly emotional issue active in this country. This is the issue of feticide that is euphemistically called abortion in order to obscure the true nature of the act.

Strange as it may seem from a logical or rational point of view, those in Group A, opposing gun control, also tend to oppose feticide. On the other hand, those in Group B, favoring gun control, tend to favor feticide.

This *pairing* of these positions has been well substantiated by published commentaries and opinion polls. It is a fact that deaths by feticide far outnumber firearm related homicides.[106] The reader can decide which group holds irrationally contradictory beliefs.

There seems to be conflicting realities between *what-is* and *what-should-be*. Beliefs based on *what-should-be* a type of fantasy are and can be the root cause of much confusion and incorrect notions. Also, all too often these short-sighted objectives have long term negative impact.

On the other hand, although seeing reality from the *what-is* point of view is more rational, too much of this notion might also stifle needed changes. Maintaining a strict *what-is* preference should not be an inflexible clinging to the status quo and those with the strong *what-should-be* mind-set should attempt to face realities and strive for a notion closer to *what-is,* in the sense of rational acceptance of reality.

It should be remembered that action and belief are inextricably connected such that even a private belief, which might appear trivial and of no significance, still influences behavior.

It seems that many individuals are not able to accept, or even recognize, the difference between these two notions. This problem seems most prevalent when dealing with highly emotional issues such as religion, culture, and politics. Inflexible adherence to any position is not a good thing, there needs to be a balance.

There are also some beliefs that may be considered a working hypothesis where complete and full verification is yet to come such that how and when such verification might occur is open and not capable of prior determination. Perhaps, it will come as a dramatic and sudden

---

[106] More than half a million feticides occur in the US each year (2014 data), while the firearm homicide rate has declined. The FBI estimated 13,455 firearm homicides for 2015 (this number is up from 2014, but down from 2006).

illumination, but more likely, it will come in increments, which eventually accumulate sufficiently to achieve acceptance.

Language

What is language? The simple answer is; it is how we communicate. Language, for humans, is a combination of spoken and written symbols, facial expressions, images (pictures), and what is commonly called *body language*.

When communicating, and we are always communicating in some manner either consciously or subconsciously, we use these elements of language in various combinations and degrees of emphasis.

Cultural content is deeply embedded in all languages and the two cannot be separated. Even when it is commonly supposed that two cultures speak the same language, each culture has specific language nuances, some subtle and others not so subtle. One only needs to recall the well-known aphorism that 'England and the USA are two countries separated by a common language.'

Language is the association of abstract objects (words, both written and spoken) with concrete objects (physical things), abstract objects (mental things), and actions (events). That is, words are conceptual symbols that represent things, thoughts, and actions that only have meaning within the context of a linguistic convention.

This convention is, in general, not a one-to-one correspondence between words and things, but a one-to-many correspondence such that a word can and often (usually?) does have multiple meanings. Consequently, we must rely on sentential context for the intended meaning.[107]

As languages evolve words often lose their original meaning but continue to be used in the same old way. For example, consider the words *sunrise* and *sunset*. Although still capable of conjuring up delightful images, most of us know that the earth rotates and that the sun only appears to *rise* and *set*.

As is well known, language variations are often based on regional and social conventions. However, less recognized (or just less discussed), is the

---

[107] For example, one of my favorites is the word *run*, which in the Random House Webster's unabridged dictionary, 2nd edition, 1987, has 179 usage definitions!

2.1 Miscellany of Preliminary Topics

fact that language is also a gauge for personal judgment. How an individual uses language is an indicator of their education, personality, social situation, and world-view.

Richness of vocabulary or the lack of richness and the excessive use of slang, colloquialisms, or profanity are personal indicators that say much about ourselves and play a key role in determining how we are perceived by others.

A few decades ago, it was common to hear quotes from literature and poetry, but, today, most often all we hear are catchy phrases from popular movies or television sit-coms that usually don't have much depth of meaning.

Explanations and Perception

At first, explanations may not seem closely related to historical writing; however, since the general purpose of an explanation is to transfer information there is a clear connection with how events are perceived.

Anyway, we spend a lot more time explaining than we imagine and probably think less about the quality of these explanations than we should. There can be no doubt that the quality of an explanation has considerable bearing on how we understand something and that in turn affects us perceptually.

The motivations for explanations seem to have two main purposes; they are intended to instruct (inform) or they are attempts to persuade (influence) – or both. Either way, it is possible to divide explanations into three common types; by *example*, by *labeling*, and by *instruction*.

The *example* type can be further divided into two subtypes, called *like-example* explanations and *specific-example* explanations.

Explanations of the *like-example* type, use examples of objects with similar properties, but these objects are different from that being explained. This type is used frequently when attempting to clarify an event or object where a known specific example does not exist or is unknown.

For example, it is said that rattlesnake meat looks like fish and tastes like chicken. What this type of explanation is really doing is using familiar examples to create a sort of sensory boundary around the object of the explanation and provide a sensory image based on the similarities.

Although this type of explanation is enough for everyday situations, it definitely lacks accuracy. On the other hand, the *specific-example* type of explanation attempts to explain using examples of the object of explanation.

For example, a small clock attached to a wrist by a small band uses specific features of this type of clock. The obvious difference is, rattlesnake meat is not chicken or fish, but a wristwatch is a small clock and attaches with a small band.

The *labeling* type is the weakest of the three. For example, while shopping in a grocery store, I queried a store clerk about an unfamiliar fruit. The clerk's answer was to provide the name of the fruit. Obviously, simply naming the fruit, or anything else, is not an explanation.

The *instruction* type, as the name implies, involves a list of instructions, and can be broken down into two subtypes of either *operational* or *functional* explanations. The *operational* explanation might also be called the *recipe type* explanation. Although helpful, a list of instructions really does not explain much at all, it merely provides a series of steps. Instructions for making a cake tell us little about the cake itself.

On the other hand, the *functional* explanation is one that includes the *why-how* or the *cause-effect*. That is, it is not just a list of instructions, but a true explanation, which provides reasons or justifications for the actions.

The point is that the quality and manner of explanations directly influence our perceptions, especially when, as is often the case, the explanation is an attempt to influence the recipient.

Such explanations are common in commercial and political advertisements. Both types of advertisements use misleading statements and incomplete information in their attempts to influence opinions. They only pretend to be informational, while actually attempting to influence rather than inform.

Errors of omission, purposeful or otherwise, are a common way to make both products and politicians seem more favorably. For example, product commercials frequently use statements such as *15% less* or *doctors recommend* which are meaningless without knowledge of the alleged context.

These and similar *context-less* statements are common in product advertising, while in politics, we frequently hear vague and broad

2.1 Miscellany of Preliminary Topics

statements about *making things better* or *helping the middle class*. Here, the omissions are usually the specific ways and means of accomplishing what is promised.

Such statements never really explain what the actual process of improvement might be or how things will get better. Without doubt, the producers of these misleading statements are experts at obfuscation, ambiguity, amphiboly, and so on.

We should remember that manipulation of our perception is the business of advertising and they are very good at their business. All advertising has a visible agenda, and it should be assumed there is also a hidden or unvisible agenda.

Side Comment on the Power of a Single Word: The Nicene Creed, first published in the year 325, evolved over time and by the 15th century, the Western Catholic Church, and the Eastern Orthodox Church had different versions of this creed. The Catholic version contained the Latin word 'filioque', which translates as 'and from the son.' The Orthodox version of the creed did not contain this word.

Consequently, in an age of strong religious ardor, this difference was enough to cause a rift between these two Christian sects such that, in 1453, when Constantinople, the center of Eastern Orthodoxy, was under siege by the Ottoman Empire, the Christian West would not send aid to the Christian East. The result was the capture of Constantinople and the history of Europe and Asia were changed forever. Never underestimate the power of a single word!

Symbolic versus Intimate Knowledge
This section borrows from Sir Arthur Eddington (English, 1882-1944) the notion that there are two basic forms of knowledge; *symbolic knowledge* and *intimate knowledge*.[108]

Symbolic knowledge is associated with reasoning and analysis, while intimate knowledge resists reasoning and analysis, and if submitted to analysis ceases being intimate knowledge. For example, Eddington used humor as an example of intimate knowledge. When a joke is submitted to analysis it loses humor, ceases being *intimate*, and becomes *symbolic*.

---

[108] Arthur S. Eddington, *The Nature of the Physical World*: Gifford Lectures (Newcastle upon Tyne, UK: Cambridge Scholars Publishing, 1927), 286.

Not surprisingly, the world of scientific and technical investigations lies in the realm of symbolic knowledge and this knowledge is applicable only within that world. The worlds of passion, value, and purpose all lie in the domain of intimate knowledge. Mysticism and spirituality are also types of intimate knowledge and it is a category mistake to apply scientific analysis to such topics.

Although mysticism and spirituality are within the domain of intimate knowledge, theology, which sets the *rules* for ritual and behavior, is symbolic knowledge. This is why those who practice a particular doctrine too closely often become inflexible and intolerant. [As the above side comment on the power of a single word illustrated, the devil is in the dogmatic details.]

This separation of symbolic and intimate knowledge does not mean that intimate knowledge, such as spirituality is without symbols; on the contrary, symbols play a significant role in matters of the spirit and other categories of intimate knowledge. These, however, are not the symbols of science such as the symbolic models of mathematics and measurement.

Spiritual symbols are instilled with emotional conviction and the mystical. Such symbols remind us of those moments of connection with the natural world that are often forgotten during the mundane routines of everyday life.

It is an unfortunate person who is incapable of feeling this sanctioned urge or striving for that which transcends symbolic knowledge. Whether triggered by some natural phenomenon or by some sudden insight, this experience of the intimate knowledge of spirituality and mysticism is unhindered by the world of symbolic knowledge and is a realization of the striving within the human spirit for true enlightenment.

Sensory Pollution

"Put a man into a perfect chaos of phenomena, sights, sounds, feelings; and if the man continued to exist, and to be rational at all, his attention would doubtless soon find for him a way to make up some kind of rhythmic regularity, which he would impute to the things about him, so as to imagine that he had discovered some law of sequence in this mad new world."[109]

---

[109] Josiah Royce, *The Religious Aspects of Philosophy* (Boston and New York: Houghton Mifflin Company, 1885), 317.

2.1 Miscellany of Preliminary Topics

This quote, from a work published in 1885, seems very modern. The author was living in Boston at that time, and, as anyone who has ever been to Boston can attest, the chaos of the 1885 that inspired this comment has surely increased greatly since then. Given this and Royce's rather bucolic background, this sensitivity to the seeming chaos of Boston is not surprising.[110] Of course, this is not just a Boston phenomenon, but because of increasing urbanization and industrialization this is exactly what we now experience in every urban environment.

Today, besides urbanization, the development of various technological appliances has enabled and facilitated constant sensory bombardment. Just as urban illumination (light pollution) has all but eliminated the once magnificent nightly stellar spectacle, auditory pollution has smothered the sounds of nature.

As if this pollution is not bad enough, we commonly see individuals who seem unable to function without something plugged into their ears, and thereby, substitute one form of auditory pollution for another of their choosing.

An adjunct to this increase in sensory pollution appears to be a growing need for over stimulation and constant entertainment that combine to form a closed loop of escalating excessive stimulation.

This seems especially true in current cinema where special effects and loudness are, at an increasing rate, replacing dialog and story. The use of computer-generated graphics is replacing natural scenery, and this stimulates a striving for even more visual stimulation. At the same time, monster sound systems blast ever louder.

Of course, such excess is not new; this trend of loudness and spectacle has long plagued popular music, where voice augmentation, ear breaking audio, and visual overload are the norm. This constant and excessive sensory stimulation affects perception through over stimulation, which leads to desensitization.

One result of all this pollution is the alteration of our perception of what constitutes entertainment itself. Entertainment has moved from a form of

---

[110] Josiah Royce (American philosopher, 1855-1916) was born, in the small foothill town of Grass Valley, California.

relaxation, reflection, and even edification to a form of extreme exaggeration and sensory excess that is all but devoid of meaningful content.[111]

Sensitivity?

When we say that a person is sensitive, it commonly has either of two meanings. It might mean that this person is empathetically sensitive to the feelings of others or is a statement about a person who is easily offended, easily embarrassed, or otherwise emotionally fragile. The problem is that it is easy to confuse these two when someone refers rather ambiguously to someone as being *sensitive*.

Then there is also a sensitivity of a third type, this is the sensitivity of awareness. For example, in the case of perceptual sensitivity it means awareness of subtleties such as body language and facial expressions, not just the spoken word. How you respond to others and how others respond to you is often determined by observing and understanding the less obvious differences and similarities.

Too Much Technology?

Is it possible to have too much technology? Is there a point where the benefits of technology peak and start being overshadowed by the downside?

First, here are some of the benefits of technology. These benefits include more leisure time, longer life expectancy, creature comforts, almost instant worldwide communications, and so on.

Ok, so what are some of the downside effects of technology? These include a considerable increase in the number of persons unable to care for themselves, increase in government control, loss of privacy, almost instant worldwide communications, and so on.

Wait a minute, wasn't *almost instant worldwide communications* listed both as a pro and a con? Faster communication can and does have many benefits, but at present, it seems that the main use of this ubiquitous communications capability is the transmission of trivialities. There is no

---

[111] Additionally, it should be mentioned that in cinema there seems to be a trend toward apocalyptic scenarios and myriads of super-heroes with outlandish powers. Together these trends seem to indicate a certain fatalistic pessimism and a strong desire to escape into fantasy.

2.1 Miscellany of Preliminary Topics

doubt that Facebook, Twitter, and the other so-called *social* media systems are mostly full of idle chatter with little substance and a tendency toward self-aggrandizement.

In recent years, there have been *technology-induced* changes in social behavior that have developed in a steady and, at first, subtle manner. For example, the development of personal communication devices, in combination with the so-called *social* media has changed the way people communicate with each other. These addictive devices provide the appearance of bringing people closer together, while, in practice, more often they separate people by being *inwardly* focused and not *outwardly* focused.

More properly, this phenomenon should be called *anti-social* media. As for *bringing people together*, it appears that the opposite is true. A common café or restaurant scene is two or more persons sitting at the same table and all are using their devices to communicate with absent parties while essentially ignoring their actual companions.

It is argued that these addictive personal communication devices and social media in general provide a useful and meaningful way to communicate with distant friends and relatives. To some extent, this is true, but is it necessary to follow every move someone makes? Do we really need to know what everyone had for lunch, pictures of animals in human garb, or endless selfies?

There seems little doubt, that the great advances in technology have given us the false impression that humanity has also made progress in solving pressing social and economic problems. Unfortunately, this is not the case; our cleverness in technology has clearly outpaced any progress in other areas of human concern and need.

The internet and personal communication devices have given us a world of information at our fingertips but has also not provided us with as much useful knowledge as might be assumed. It appears that most of these communication resources are used for on-line shopping, social media, and so on, instead of more useful endeavors.

The machine, especially the computer, which is a purely syntax device, devoid of semantics, seems to have become the new idol. It is interesting and somewhat prophetic that the pure syntax computer has come to such prominence over the last few decades. It seems to fit perfectly into a society that prefers syntax (form, posturing) over semantics (content, meaning, action).

Self-expression has increasingly taken the place of achievement. This is seen especially true within the realm of popular entertainment where it is becoming more common for someone becoming *famous for being famous*. A culture of posturing is rapidly replacing the culture of correct behavior, personal integrity, and accomplishment.

Examples include the phenomena of affecting a certain fad and pretend accomplishments like walking to cure something, but really to get a t-shirt. As another example, it should be noted that *raising awareness* is not really an accomplishment, it is an inwardly focused gesture.

There is also the trend that seems to be attempting to place everyone on the same level, which is essentially an attempt to push down high achievers as opposed to bring up low achievers. Education seems more occupied with lowering standards than raising up achievement levels of marginalized students.

Today students don't quote Shakespeare or other classical writers and poets, they quote lyrics from pop song and dialog from cinemas. We have also forgotten that, equality, under the law, does not mean all are identical or of equal capability, or motivation.

Perhaps, it is not that we have too much technology, maybe we just have too much of the wrong use of technology.

The Unexpected
It is an unfortunate truth, that within the affairs of humans, nothing ever happens exactly according to plan or as intended. Things always turn out different. This does not mean that goals are never achieved, but that within the complexity of social life, there is always the unexpected and we never get exactly the intended result.

These unforeseen consequences are also an essential problem within *social science*. Even best efforts to foresee these unwanted events and results are never completely successful, only degrees of success less than 100% are always achieved. This phenomenon is so common that it is often overlooked or not recognized as an intrinsic property of social affairs.

In part, the unexpected is a result of complexity and the lag between cause and effect such that only later do these unforeseen events and results

2.1 Miscellany of Preliminary Topics

become known. The examples are so many, it is difficult to choose only a few of examples, but here are three that seems representative.

Example 1 is common within the information technology field. After extensive testing and simulations, major projects often fail on going *live* or into productive use because of unexpected and unforeseen conditions.

The author is personally familiar with the case where a large corporation developed a new stockholder's records system that was developed and tested over many months, but the first time it was use for *real* it failed because the designers had not expected to cut a dividend check greater than $999,999.99. And that caused the system to fail.

Example 2 is the well-known phenomena of political upsets, where a strongly (supposed) favorited candidate does not win.

Example 3? I will leave that to the reader to select. The essential point is; there is always the unexpected!

Cause and Effect
"The first step is just the observation that, in most cases, what persuades us of the reality of some fact, existence, or presence is reasoning based on a cause-and-effect relationship."[112]

The notion of cause and effect is so common, that we tend to either overlook the process altogether or assume cause and effect relations where there is little or no direct evidence that supports this notion. Cause and effect can be as obvious as the breaking of a dropped glass or as subtle as finding your shoes where you left them. In the latter case, the effect was delayed for some time after the cause, while in the former example effect followed cause in quick succession.

If the gap between the cause and the effect is short, making the connection between cause and effect is usually simplified, but if there is a significant delay, then making the connection between cause and effect can be problematic up to the point of being unresolvable. Moreover, when the delay is extensive, possible causes are many, and, possibly, not all causes are known, then the connections between cause and effect can be problematic to the extreme.

---

[112] Bernard d'Espagnat, *Veiled Reality* (Reading, MA: Addison-Wesley 1995), 10.

The truth is that our ability to determine cause and effect is very limited. Only within relatively simple situations can we effectively determine cause and effect. As soon as we move into the complex realms of organic life, the human mind, world ecology, and social dynamics our ability to make true and effective cause and effect connections declines rapidly to the point of being guess work.

Anyway, there is a comfort factor and strong satisfaction in establishing cause and effect relations about something. That is, there is something in the human psyche that seems to drive us to find cause and effect connections.

Dynamic Accommodation
Throughout our lives, we are constantly acquiring new knowledge of the world. Even though we execute most of our daily rituals without much thought, in a subtle but very real sense, every time we perform, even a routine task, it is a new experience. Things have changed between each repetition of the experience. All sorts of things have occurred, and the world has moved on.

For example, I visited the same coffee house this morning that I visited yesterday, but today's trip was different from yesterday's trip in a number of ways. The traffic was different, different people came into the coffee house, and so on.

Today, like all days, is similar and yet different from yesterday and every other day. The differences are only slightly noticed and the same can be said about the similarities. That is, in the course of our lives, similar-differences and different-similarities are generally overlooked or given little overt thought, if any.

This is because as we go about our daily lives, we dynamically accommodate these subtle changes without giving them any thought or notice. Unless we encounter an event, which is traumatic or in some other way unusual, we tend to ignore subtle changes and in doing so, we accommodate these changes and receive emotional comfort through familiarity and the maintenance of normalcy.

Intersubjective Agreement
There is a class of agreements within societies that are a part of socially constructed reality and are based on implicitly recognized common

2.1 Miscellany of Preliminary Topics

agreements. These agreements can be as limited as an agreement between two persons or as broad as an agreement encompassing whole societies.

An intersubjective agreement is a collaboration and corroboration between individuals, which exists by extension within communities and societies in general. This type of agreement, in conjunction with the previously discussed dynamic accommodation, is not only essential for normal functioning, but is an essential element of societies and nations.

These intersubjective agreements are usually non-binding; it relies mostly on common understandings, social conventions, and are not governed by legal statutes. For example, at the level of societies, these types of agreements govern what is considered proper behavior or tacit agreements of confidence in certain aspects of society, such as confidence in the honesty of the election process, and the observance of locally accepted social practices.

At the more personal level, married couples frequently rely on this type of agreement, although in this case, the agreement might be considered binding.

Moreover, these agreements often serve as a reinforcement or confirmation of believed reality and provide a level of assurance that one's reality is also that of the collective.

Groupthink

Groupthink should not be confused with intersubjective agreements. Groupthink is a practice within collectives that determine the group's dynamics and ideologies, and often, allow little or no flexibility as to when someone is permitted to deviate from the group theme or consensus.

This is the practice that most of us believe is characteristic of restrictive political systems or militant organizations that allow little or no freedom of individual expression or deviation from official dogma.

However, this is only partially true, groupthink is prominent in societies and organizations that are generally considered open and free, and might include just about any collective association, such as corporations, political parties, religious entities, and social identification.

Here is a short list, devoid of details, of some of the primary symptoms of groupthink:

- Unquestioned adherence to the group's ideology.
- Unquestioned belief in the morality of the group's acts and beliefs.
- Rejection of any information that might conflict with stated positions.
- Opponents are considered too naïve or ignorant to appreciate the group's policies and opinions.
- Illusion of unanimity within the group and the false notion that silence is consent.
- Direct and often coercive pressure on dissenters.
- Certain individuals take on the role of true-believers, enforcers, and protectors of the group.

Perhaps, after scanning this list, the reader might recognize that perhaps they too are a member of some groupthink association. Or possibly they might believe that this list belongs to *other people* and certainly not oneself! Of course, this list is not inclusive, and not all item listed are necessary for groupthink to exist.[113] Only two or three items may be sufficient for the existence of groupthink.

There is also the question of how many members of a group must agree to a commitment such that it becomes a group commitment? Other than the simple *it depends* answer, there is no simple or definite answer. Group hierarchy would naturally play a role as would how vocal are the supporters of a commitment. Strong leadership versus roll call voting are also considerations.

Within every group, committee, or social aggregate there exists the group agenda that is public, the individual agendas of group members, and hidden agendas. When it comes to group dynamics, all members are never equally weighted: 1) There are always groups leaders, implicitly or explicitly. 2) There are always members who are stronger and/or more vocal, and 3) there are those members along for the ride.

It should also be noted, that groupthink can apply where there is no formal organization but only a life-style or other affectation that has followers who indorse and adopt the collective lifestyle. For example, those who follow a certain fad or effect a certain mode of dress or overall appearance.

---

[113] Those interested should consult: Janis, I. L. (1972). *Groupthink: psychological studies of policy decision and fiascos.* Boston, MA: Houghton Mifflin.

2.1 Miscellany of Preliminary Topics

Truth and Validity
It seems that there are three main types or categories of truth. First are the truths that are synonymous with 'fact.' For example, all humans are mortal. The second type is the pronouncement of a veridical belief, such as, the earth revolves around the Sun. In this case, truth matches reality although not directly observed and is an example of intersubjective agreement. Most scientific truths are of this second type.

The third type of truth is somewhat different; it is the acceptance of truth without proof, such as the acceptance of spiritual knowledge and awareness as reality. Testimonial truth, or rather testimony that we deem to be true, falls into this third type.

Sometimes the word truth is mistakenly used as a synonym for validity, while the fact of the matter is that a statement may be logically valid, but untrue. Validity, logically speaking, is about form (syntax), while truth is about content (semantics). For example, consider the well-known syllogism: All men are mortal, Socrates is a man, and, therefore, Socrates is mortal. These statements are both valid and true.

On the other hand, consider these statements: All unicorns have a single horn, Narwhals have a single horn, and, therefore, Narwhals are unicorns. In each example, the first two statements are premises and the third is the conclusion. Although both examples are logically valid, in the first example, the first two statements (premises) are true and the conclusion is true, while in the second example, the two premises are true (in the case of the unicorn abstractly true), but the conclusion is not true.

There are several reasons why the second example is untrue, but the main one is a category mistake. The unicorn is in the category of fictitious creatures, while the Narwhal is in the category of real creatures. This common type of mistake is often used on purpose by advertising agencies.

Advertisers will present what appears a true and valid argument for their product, but the argument is not true because of a category mistake such as the miss-matched premises in the second example. Logical validity is about following the rules, while truth is about meaning.

2.2 Contemporary History: A Commentary

In what follows, I have attempted to bring forward and discuss how certain social trends have influenced not only contemporary historical writings but are also having strong influence on how certain segments of society now see reality. We need to remember that the manner in which current events are presented by the news media along with contemporary writings on social and political issues will become the sources for historians of the future.

To be sure, we all, to some extent, modify objective perception and veridical reality to be more agreeable with our world-view but, today, this has become more extreme such that there seems to be a real issue of imbalance in contemporary historical writings.

Unfortunately, today, in addition to personal agendas of selective emphasis and exclusion, there is a trend among some historians to change historical perspectives through various practices such as *contextual displacement*, which is using today's standards of social measurement to judge the past, and by extension, bring blame for injustices forward to the present with the implication that elements of today's society are still responsible for these past injustices.

2.2 Contemporary History

Reconsidering Reality

"Physical reality, then, is the realm of actual and possible sense perceptions. The concretely physical is just that which yields and sustains perceptual experiences."

"The belief in physical reality is really, in a final analysis, belief in a public realm of experience, accessible to other percipients of like nature with one's self. This belief, therefore, rests on the recognition of a social realm of beings with the same perceptual and rational powers."[114]

"The aim of the whole process seems to be to reach as complete and united a conception of reality as possible, a conception wherein the greatest fullness of data shall be combined with the greatest simplicity of conception. The effort of consciousness seems to be to combine the greatest richness of content with the greatest definiteness of organization."[115]

As the above quotes state, our reality has both personal and collective aspects. That is, reality based on personal experience of the world as presented and interpreted by our senses and on community agreement.

Since perception is the primary source of our reality, understanding perception is necessary if we are to understand our reality. Experience of the external world through accumulation and assimilation of sensations forms the basis for reality. The experiences of external sensations are expanded through the mental processes of classification, induction, deduction, inference, and so on. Although, not completely reliable, these processes are the only way we gain knowledge of the external world.

Besides the word reality, we also use the word *actual* to designate what we feel is real. However, the word actual has a somewhat different usage, as it is often used to emphasis current existence, a recent occurrence, or an immediate presence. For example, statements such as 'I was actually there.' indicate an emphasis on being personally present.

Consider also the words reality and real. Reality is the world of phenomena and our perception, real is the world behind the phenomena and

---

[114] First two quotes: J. A Leighton, "Perception and Physical Reality." *The Philosophical Review, Vol. 19, No. 1* (Jan. 1910), pp. 1-21, Published by: Duke University Press on behalf of Philosophical Review, URL: http://www.jstor.org/stable/2177636, 10, 16.

[115] Josiah Royce *Mind and Reality* (1882), https://archive.org/details/mindreality00roycrich, 357.

perception. Reality is the thing as perceived, real is the thing-in-itself, which is both unknown and unknowable.

Types of Reality

Within the technical literature, of the type that discusses such things, we encounter a plethora of realities and realisms. Each was conceived to meet a perceived need and each type of reality has subscribers in agreement with that realism.

Having said that, a reader believing in only one kind of reality might be inclined to object. Certainly, on the surface it seems that only one reality, often called common (or naive) reality, exists. However, when we dig deeper into what we normally consider *reality*, we find that it does have many variations.

In no particular order, here is a short, but representative sampling of the various realism that might be encountered; Conceptual Realism, Scientific Realism, Conventional Realism, Platonic Realism, Empirical Realism, Common Realism, and Operational Realism. This list could go on, but as an example it is enough to get across the idea that there is no fixed – one size fits all – reality.

The events in our lives manifest themselves in distinct, but connected, ways. The natural world of phenomena is objectively presented; however, our interpretation and contemplation of these events is partly subjective and individually unique. Neither the natural phenomena nor our interpretation can be avoided and together they determine our version of reality.

When the objective experience, the phenomenal events common to all, and the subjective interpretation meet certain cultural and social conventions, then the observer is said to be normal within the constraints and conventions common to the observer's culture.

Stated simply, reality has a certain amount of variability, which depends on such things as individual capabilities, knowledge, social environment, inclination, and so on. To illustrate this point, here is an example of two very different realities.

In the Kalahari Desert of southwest Africa, reside the native Bushmen (San People) who, from the point of view of environment, technology, and formal education, live very primitive lives. Indeed, until recently, these people had lives not far removed from what we commonly call stone-age humanity.

At the other extreme are the typical young urban dwellers, perhaps living in Los Angeles or London, who are constantly connected to the latest technical gadgets, especially those starting with 'i'. These various technical accoutrements tend to be constant companions of urban living in general and youthful urban living in particular.

On the other hand, the *advanced* technology of the Bushmen is fire generated by wood friction and a bow and arrows. These individuals live in habitats about as far apart, regarding both social environment and technology, as is possible these days.

The native desert dwellers, although technologically primitive, have an intimate alignment with the natural world, which includes not only physical objects, but also includes a strong transcendent spiritual sensibility and an awareness of the integrated wholeness of existence.

On the other hand, the urban dweller, technologically over equipped and spiritually deprived, is mainly occupied with technology and a certain social behavior mediated by current fashion.

One is fully integrated into the natural world, while the other is fully integrated into the world of artifacts and superficiality. It is not hard to imagine that each have a very different view of reality. What one is missing, the other has in abundance.[116]

To be sure, we do not have to go to such extremes to find variations in reality; each of us has a personal view that is never exactly the same as that of another. For example, two persons viewing the same rainbow will probably have different interpretations of the event.

A meteorologist, for example, will look beyond the phenomenon and see not only the rainbow, but will reflect on the physical causes of rainbows. On the other hand, an artist will most likely see the esthetics of the rainbow. Which interpretation is the *real* one? Of course, both are just as real for each person.

---

[116] Unfortunately, the government of Botswana has re-located many of the Bushmen, and their old way of living is quickly fading.

Reality is partially based on our assumption and belief in veridical perception. That is, perception considered to be truthful or coinciding with reality. As the observer's knowledge becomes more complete, in the sense of increased insight into the observed structure and properties of the objects and events experienced, then the observer's reality is modified accordingly. Seeking knowledge and increasing understanding not only modifies individual reality, it also enhances a person's worldview.

Some say that technical knowledge blunts the edge of natural beauty and dulls one's sense of the wonders of nature. This is a misconception. For example, knowing something about what generates a rainbow can and will enhance the observer's appreciation of the wonder of this phenomenon. It is nature bringing together the right structure and composition at the right time to produce a thing of beauty.

Knowledge enhances the capacity to *see* beyond the common perceptual perspective of things and perceive the wonders of nature with more depth and understanding. This acquisition of knowledge is different from the over use and dependence on technical accoutrements as discussed above. Dependence or addiction is not knowledge.

Perceptual consistency is fundamental to our notions of external reality. This consistency is achieved through the continuous correlation of active sensations with past sensations. This process is more than the mere collection of data but includes processing the data into information and information into knowledge.

The concrescence or the objective reality of an external object is most strongly determined through perceptual persistence and consistency. Multiple encounters with the same or similar objects reinforce the concept of the existence of a particular object and in this way, the external world as projected into us is integrated with our sense of self to form the totality of our reality.

All versions of reality, at least those considered rational, are built on a fundamental and unalterable basis of all realities. This basis of reality includes, for example, unalterable and unavoidable components of reality such as the irrepressible force of gravity, the limits to biological existence, biological necessities such as sustenance, and so on. This basis necessarily forms the foundation of all variations of rational reality.

Given this unavoidable basis or foundation, one might question whether these *variations of reality* are nothing more than mental exercises. However,

2.2 Contemporary History

there can be no doubt that since we pattern our lives on our personal worldview, these variations must be considered a part of our reality.

On reaching adulthood, we are, for the most part, set in our ways and have established a reality for ourselves, which influences all our activities and opinions. Although it is possible for a person to modify their worldview somewhat and suppress certain behaviors or features of their reality, a full escape is probably not possible.

At the inner most level, our personal reality is deeply ingrained such that changes are difficult or even impossible. We can change cosmetically or superficially, but just as the topiary designer may change its outer appearance, the bush is still the same bush, similarly, the person's basic nature remains.

Influences on Contemporary History

Sources and Veracity of Information

Years past, communities were more isolated and necessarily relied on local expertise for trusted testimony. In this country, up until the implementation of improved means of communication, it used to be the family doctor, the local clergy, or other individuals of authority who were by default, and close proximity, the primary sources of information and judgment.

Prior to ready access to printed material and the existence of a high percentage of literacy, the main source of information was the verbal testimony of others. This indicates that for the most part traditional information transfer was a social activity in the sense that information was transferred directly from one person to another.

Today, it is more likely that the sources of information are televised news reports, posts on *social* media, and other largely unsubstantiated sources, which are indirect and removed from our personal environment.

Enabling technology has extended the sources of testimony to include a plethora of sources that provide an overload of verbal, written, and pictorial sources of information. However, within this plethora of sources and types of media, testimony-based information varies greatly in credence and veracity. It seems that with more sources and more options, these sources of information have become less reliable. Perhaps, a quantitative glut inevitably leads to a qualitative decline.

However, human nature seems to dictate that regardless of the source, unless we have some knowledge or belief that questions the speaker's reliability, we tend to accept testimonies without proof of reliability. In short, by default, we are trusting.

On the other hand, if we know, or believe, that the speaker has been untruthful in the past, no matter the topic, then we will tend to discount all subsequent statements, regardless of the topic, and this rejection will last until such time as the speaker is able to reestablish our faith in their trustfulness.

As access to information has increased, so has the breadth of expertise narrowed. The age of the natural philosopher (polymath) is all but over and, necessarily, the age of specialization is becoming more pronounced. This means that we are all becoming more dependent on the testimony of others, while at the same time, because of certain social trends, the veracity of testimony is more suspect than ever before.

Of these various sources of information, perhaps the least reliable are the social media sources such as Facebook and Twitter. Both sources offer up a wealth of misinformation, counterfactuals, and just plain lies.

Just because someone posted something on Facebook as being factual, certainly doesn't make it so. As for the myth of *bringing people together*, just the opposite is true. Instead of *social* media, it should be called *isolation* or *anti-social* media. [See *Too Much Technology* page 145]

Then there are services such as Wikipedia that offers information through thousands of anonymous articles on just about everything. Such services should only be used when a person has some prior knowledge and seeks memory refreshment or possible informational corroboration. Although much, if not most, of the Wikipedia content is reasonably factual, cross-checking with other sources is always a good idea. This is especially true for political or other highly emotional content.

Quite obviously, our capability for obtaining first-hand experience is very limited, and by necessity, we must rely on the testimony of others. That is, we are forced, at least tentatively, to accept some testimony of some others.

The power and scope of the internet and associated media applications puts a wealth of information, literally, at our finger tips, but with no guarantee of accuracy. There seems little doubt that making the determination between expert opinion and false, or overly biased, opinion is a challenge that, unfortunately, has no absolute solution.

It seems that the news media providers think it is their duty to dilute, alter, or withhold altogether news that they feel inappropriate or uncomfortable. This allows the media to emphasis events that they deem newsworthy in order to guide the beliefs of the audience in a manner compatible with the media's preferred social agendas, and for events that don't meet their beliefs, they simply fail to report.

For sure, selective reporting and agenda motivated reporting, has been going on for as long as anyone can remember and will continue into the future. For example, the slogan *All the news that is fit to print.* was the motto of the New York Times newspaper empire over a hundred years ago, and, of course, they were the ones who decided what was fit.

Also, there is a long tradition of news media endorsing political candidates and to generally favor one political party over the other. In the glory days of newspapers, such endorsements by media giants, such as Hearst, would often make or break a candidate's chances of election.[117]

However, something has changed over the last few decades and especially since 2000 or so. The news media has moved from merely favoring one or the other party to positions of extreme polarization in their alignment with one party over another.

It seems obvious that the various news media sources engage in *information patronizing* and *censorship*. They do this by selecting what they want us to see, hear, or read, based on specific social agendas. Such ideologically biased news, although not a new thing, is more pervasive than before and more extreme in opinions concerning what they choose to report.

There seems little doubt that this polarization has intensified over the last decade or so. With only rare exceptions, public media sources in the US have aligned themselves with a particular political party to such a degree that attitudes of most media sources have moved beyond simple favoritism and are now openly hostile toward the party they do not favor.[118]

Information Deprivation

"Cassius: The fault, dear Brutus, is not in our stars, but in ourselves..."[119]

Information deprivation can be loosely defined as a condition or situation when a person or social group is deemed to be unfairly deprived of information because of lack of access to education and other epistemic resources. Often, it is claimed to be a deprivation of access to information resources due to social bias or ethnic exclusion.

---

[117] Here is an example of how the old newspaper empires could influence US society. In 1898, the U. S. Battleship, Maine was sunk by a mysterious explosion while anchored in the Havana, Cuba harbor. The Hearst newspaper chain claimed that the explosion was an act of terrorism against the USA. This claim was enough to sway public opinion and the result was the Spanish-American War. Only years later, was it revealed that the sinking was caused by an accidental internal explosion, not by an act of terrorism.

[118] Now there is the new term fake news, which is really just a euphemism for lying if intentional or spreading counterfactuals and bad journalism if unintentional.

[119] William Shakespeare. *Julius Caesar* (I, ii, 140-141)

2.2 Contemporary History

In the US, this often comes out as an accusation that the US educational system is biased in favor of those of European descent, and that culturally different minority groups are systemically penalized because of the techniques and standards used by the educational system.

Put another way, there is an opinion that when it comes to information access there are sub-cultures[120] within the US (and the world at large) who have marginalized access to epistemic resources.

I can't speak for the rest of the world, but, in the US, this is partially because of economics, partially because of social priorities, and in some cases by choice. For example, in some sub-cultures social media and pop-culture might be acceptable, while seeking information and education in general are not priorities.

There seems to be the notion that different sub-cultures need different learning environments. This in turn has, over the last few decades, led to the establishment of, what are euphemistically called, *Epistemically Virtuous Institutions*.

In the US educational system, this notion of epistemically virtuous institutions, as implemented, is a dilution of educational standards in a process that has been ongoing for many years. It is a policy where textbooks are *simplified* in language and structure in the belief that this provides a means of helping marginalized groups achieve more. In effect, this term is a process for lowering standards such as grammatically correct spoken and written language usage.

As stated, some say that it is the fault of the educational system, which they claim is biased in favor of white society and uses methods that are unsuited for sub-cultures. This opinion ignores the reality that students either from Asia or of Asian descent do quite well within the existing system in spite of the fact that many of these students have considerable cultural differences from those of European descent.

If a sub-culture places a priority on education, then there is likely to be more real learning and enhanced chances of improving one's standard of living. On the other hand, if the priorities are about pop-culture, sports, and sub-cultural identification, then the chances of improving one's standard of living are much less.

---

[120] Herein, sub-culture is not just a reference to race, but rather a reference to cultural differences such as life-style choices, educational interest, socio-economics, and so on.

Celebrities and sports figures have high visibility and even higher income, but percentage wise, they are a very small part of the total population and chances of achieving such status is, accordingly, miniscule. On the other hand, access to educational opportunities are always available to those who truly seek them.

Based on personal experience, it seems that, in the US, mediocrity is often preferred over achievement. Being a *smarty-pants* or a *dumb a__* are equally disparaged but being mediocre is ok. Put another way, the US is long on intelligence of the applied or utility sort, but very short on what might be called true intellectual inclinations.

Few attend colleges and universities to learn, they attend these institutions because they think they should or are told they should, while the majority of those who do attend seem to be only interested in getting a diploma, and, possibly, some skills that will lead to employment.

There is this social myth within the US that everyone should seek a college level education. This notion is a totally unrealistic corruption of the valid notion that everyone should have the opportunity for such an education.

A more realistic agenda would limit higher education to those who have the aptitude, capability, and aspirations that are compatible with proper goals for seeking a higher education. It seems that for most, quality of life is only an economic issue.

A consequence of this notion is the flooding of US colleges and universities with unqualified and poorly prepared students such that these institutions of *higher learning* have become more like overpriced trade or vocational schools.[121] These over-attended and over-priced institutions, stuffed with students with questionable motives and abilities, now offer watered-down degrees that really have little or no meaningful occupational possibilities.[122]

---

[121] The effects of over subscription at US colleges and universities has been higher tuitions caused by easy access to student loans. That is, easy loans have prompted schools to raise tuitions.

[122] I am always amazed at the number of employees at coffee shops such as Starbucks, who have some sort of college degree but are engaged in *non-knowledge-based* work.

2.2 Contemporary History

This is not to put down vocational and technical schools, indeed, they serve a worthy purpose and should be considered more often as ways to improve one's standard of living and as preparation for a future career.

Traditionally (to use a word that is not in current fashion) a university education was concerned with producing a better and more enlightened person and the curriculums were intellectual, not the diluted curriculum of such programs as sports management and gender studies.[123]

Testimonial Injustice[124]

Testimonial injustice is loosely defined as a listener's disbelief based not on the actual testimony, but on a pre-existing bias against the speaker for any reason. This is a form of identity bias or identity stereotyping, where, for example, the appearance of the speaker might be used as a reason to reject the speaker's testimony.

The variations of this condition are many such that they range from prejudice based only on appearance, which could include not only bodily appearance, but includes such sub-culture variables as fashion, grooming, and language usage. That is, physical appearance bias, is not just about skin color, but includes things like gender, skin modifications, various bodily adornments, choice of apparel, and language usage.

Besides appearances, there is also bias based on relationships such that a person's testimony might be disregarded. For example, sometimes only a known political or religious affiliation is all that is needed to cause testimonial rejection.

Another example, is one that I will call *testimonial injustice from ignorance*. This is the case where lack of knowledge on the listeners part causes them to discount or even ridicule testimony because they lacked appropriate knowledge or rejected the testimony because of the listener's pre-existing and conflicting belief.[125]

---

[123] Examples of traditional university curriculums includes mathematics, natural science, philosophy, medicine, and theology.

[124] Sometimes called Epistemic Injustice.

[125] On a personal note, I had the experience of writing a short essay about a family of Lynx for a 7th grade English class. The teacher gave me a very bad grade because she said that there was no animal called a Lynx. Here is a classic example of ignorance overriding legitimate testimony.

Tolerance and Free Speech

Free speech, as defined and practiced by extremists, is available only for those who agree with their radical ideology. The focus of certain radical groups seems to be about so-called *rights* instead of *responsibilities* and about *emotionalism* instead of real world *rationality*.

It seems that we never hear the word *responsibility* from certain extremists, except when talking about their opposition, who are, apparently, the only ones with responsibilities. That is, when this radical group uses the word responsibility, they seem to mean that those they oppose are responsible for most, if not all, of the ills of society, real or imagined.

True freedom of speech is not now, and never has been, a license for violence or intimidation through riotous action. Freedom of speech means freedom to express an opinion contrary to some other opinion.

It is not, and should not be, a freedom to use slander or verbally abuse, to advocate violence, or use intentional false statements. Such methods are a corruption and misuse of the 1st amendment.

Freedom without tolerance is not really *freedom,* it is the road to civil unrest. A radical minority (left or right) should not be allowed to force themselves on a society.

When masked semi-professional rioters cause disruption of free speech opportunities, and the majority of society remains silent, then that society is headed for anarchy or political tyranny. Tolerance is an indispensable ingredient of true freedom of speech.

Some radicals have a whole arsenal of slogans that they like to use against anyone who dissents from their views. These slogans include the well-worn racist card, hate-speech accusations, and now they have included the term Islamophobia, which applies negatively to anyone who states the belief that terrorists, who espouse the Islamic religion, and use this religion as a motivation or excuse for violent actions, should be called Islamic Terrorists.

And, of course, they also like to use that old fallback label of fascist or neo-Nazi, even though, I suspect, that few, if any, of those who use this term

2.2 Contemporary History

have any notion of the reality of that label. They know not its origin, nor do they know its ideology.[126]

By now, you might be wondering what all this has to do with contemporary historical writings. The answer is that the youth of America have for decades been exposed to biased versions of US history. The result is a generation that has a corrupted view of what the US stands for and have little knowledge of what makes this country a better place and how to keep a better place and improve it.

Side Comment on Left-Right Polarization: Some years ago (1961), the great logician, Kurt Gödel, wrote an essay that put forward a notion concerning the polarization between the Left and the Right.[127] The text begins with a schema of alternative philosophical world views, using the distance from theology as a sort of coordinate system.

In this schema, skepticism, materialism, and positivism stand on the Left, while spiritualism, idealism, and theology stand on the Right. This schema represents a scale where most people have elements of both extremes and are not at either extreme.

He went on to state, and rightly so, that the trend, in western society, over the last two hundred years or so has, in general, been shifting to the Left. This trend is readily apparent in the political polarization that has taken place in the US over the last few decades.

Tyranny of Imposition

The Tyranny of Imposition is. put simply, when an individual (or group) feels compelled to impose their will on society. It often has the form of an *I know what you need better than you do* attitude or a self-righteous effort to correct some assumed injustice or impose some supposed reform. They apparently believe that they know *how the world ought to be*.

Use of the phrase *ought-to-be* usually means a certain aspect of society is seen as needing reform or replacement. The problem is that society is so complex that often (usually?) a *correction,* as discussed in the above section

---

[126] On the other hand, these groups never criticize or slander totalitarian socialist or communist countries, where free speech simply does not exist.

[127] Kurt Gödel, "The Modern Development of the Foundations of Mathematics in the Light of Philosophy" *Kurt Gödel Collected Works Volume III*, Oxford UP. Oxford 1995, 374.

Reconsidering History - Part 2: Commentary

on *The Unexpected* (See page 147), has unforeseen consequences that may not become apparent for years.

For example, consider the case against the pesticide known as DDT. In 1962, Rachel Carson published a book titled *Silent Spring*. In this book, Carson blamed DDT for several environmental problems, most notably the thinning of eggs shells among certain types of birds, and subsequent decline in population of the affected species.

At that time, DDT was the most effective and widely used defense against the anopheles mosquito, which transmits deadly malarial parasites.

Although, these accusations were never fully substantiated, over the years after her publication, aided by certain environmental groups, public opinion against the use of DDT grew and eventually, in 1970, the US banned the use of DDT. Subsequently, other countries followed with their own bans such that, in effect, the ban became worldwide.

However, even now, after nearly fifty years, no other effective remedy has been put in place, and the result has been that every year hundreds of thousands, who might otherwise be save by DDT, needlessly die from malaria.

Another well-known example, is Ralph Nader's campaign against the Chevrolet Corvair. He claimed that the car was inherently unsafe – or as he put it in the title of his 1965 book; *Unsafe at Any Speed*.

His complaints were, at least, partially valid for the model years 1960 through 1963, but later models had a redesigned and much improved suspension system, which General Motors claimed to have fixed the problem that plagued the earlier models. That is, Nader's book was published after GM claims to have correctly suspension system problems two years before the book came out. But, apparently, this did not matter the book still managed to destroy the car's reputation and, before the end of the 60s, the car was out of production.

However, this book wasn't just about the Corvair, it also had scathing criticisms of the entire US automobile industry, in general. It seems that nothing in an American auto was correct, according to Nader.

After this, Nader continued to build a reputation through other condemnations, and went on to become, among certain progressive elements, something of a *folk-hero* (and occasional presidential candidate). An adjunct to this was that he demonstrated that making accusation about real or imagined problems, could be profitable. A notion that others have since followed.[128]

Rachel Carson's and Ralph Nader's true agendas are not known but given Nader's subsequent actions there seem room for doubt that his true motive was concern for the safety of Corvair owners.

It seems that action toward the rectification of social or moral injustice, or what is perceived to be a social or moral injustice, is not so much about the truth of what is asserted or the wisdom of the proposed correction. It is, often, merely an action against the *notion* of the injustice deemed by an individual (or group) to need correction, and not necessarily about factual truth.

Side Comment on Information versus Knowledge: There is a hierarchical progression where information supervenes on data and, in turn, knowledge supervenes on information. That is, we progress from sense data to information, and from information to knowledge. The acquisition of knowledge is always a comparison of new information with existing knowledge.

Put simply, sense data becomes information when it is translated into mental content, and information becomes knowledge when it is comprehended and integrated with pre-existing mental content.

Sometimes information and knowledge, as well as data, are used as synonyms. This, of course, is a mistake, although these words are somewhat connected, they are not identical in meaning, but form a cognitive hierarchy.

Social Epistemology

The word epistemology is, not a word most of us, use on a daily basis, and many, perhaps, are not exactly sure as to its meaning. That's OK, because even among those who do use this word there are many different interpretations of its exact meaning.

Some simply define epistemology as the study of knowledge and justified beliefs, and leave it at that, while others extend this definition to consider whether knowledge is an individual occupation or a collective occupation.

---

[128] For example, regardless of the veracity of his position on global warming, Al Gore has achieved considerable fame, as well as, substantial financial gain.

Still others extend this definition to include the sources of knowledge along with consideration about the credence and veracity of these sources.

To be sure, what constitutes knowledge is not that easy to define, but it is clear that followers of *Social Epistemology* (hereinafter SE) want to change what we call *knowledge*. In any case, the term SE, being a relatively new notion, also has many interpretations, which range from an individual opinion to an opinion adopted by entire social and political movements.[129]

As the word *social* might imply, practitioners of SE tend to believe that all human actions and interactions should be tempered with value-based considerations such as social agendas and, in some cases, personal agendas.

For example, many advocates of SE state that even science should include value-based considerations along with purposeful misrepresentation, and that this exclusion or modification of information from the general population is in some cases acceptable and even desirable. This notion subordinate's facts to social and personal agendas, and this, in turn, implies that it is legitimate to subordinate empirical truth (facts) in favor of social agendas.

Some SE advocates even argue that scientific facts are not discovered but manufactured. That is, science does not discover truths about the natural world, science invents them. And, strange as this may seem, this notion seems to be increasingly accepted by many scientists today, who apparently believe that epistemically inferior alternatives are allowable where goals other than advancement of knowledge are present.

Reverse this, and it means that instead of advancement of knowledge as a goal, it is legitimate for science to have goals biased by personal and social agendas that result in counterfactual[130] statements or otherwise inaccurate information.

Advocates of SE, apparently, believe that social values should play a role in essentially all human affairs, and not just science. They express the belief that such modifications and censorship are justifiable.

---

[129] Although the origin of the term social epistemology dates from the 1950's, it was not until Alvin Goldman and Steve Fuller became active in the 1980's that the term began to gain in popularity.

[130] Among other things, the term counterfactual can mean expressing a falsehood as if it were the truth – usually intentional but could be un-intentional.

2.2 Contemporary History

It must be admitted that there is some truth in these suggestions. For example, science does create conjectures about the workings of nature as a means of explaining natural phenomena.

However, these explanations, if honest, are not arbitrarily conceived and, traditionally, have been independent of social agendas. Scientific conjectures and theories are created in an effort to explain natural phenomena in a manner understandable in ordinary language, not engage in deceptive social manipulations.

For example, when a physicist speaks of an *electron*, it is a reference to a set of phenomena, which, collectively, are attributed to *some-thing* called an electron. This *phenomenal electron*, far too small for direct observation, can only be *measured* indirectly by inference and extrapolation.

That is, what we call an *electron* is the sum of a particular set of experimentally measured phenomena (data), which collectively has been given the name *electron*. The explanations of science in common language necessarily entails human interpretations, and human interpretation entails assigning symbols or names as a means of individualizing association and establishing familiarity.

Having said that, it should be noted that in the past care was taken to minimize any subjective content within a scientific conjecture or theory, but as more progressive social agendas gain in popularity, SE has become more influential and prevalent.

As a result, personal, social, and hidden agendas have become well entrenched within a type of scientific groupthink that, discouraging heterodoxy, insists on a dogmatic adherence to certain agendas that include the increased inclusion of personal and social values into scientific research and theory acceptance.[131]

Another issue is that the use of social-political values is usually not explicitly stated, and the value modified empirical content is presented as completely valid empirical evidence.

Traditional epistemic values protected testimonial integrity, while the inclusion of social-political values subordinate empirically valid data

---

[131] My book, *Space-Time (and other things) Reconsidered* discusses SE influences on contemporary science more completely. https://www.amazon.com/Space-Time-Reconsidered-Reconsideration-Perception-Reality/dp/1542368421

(facts) and are often merely a form of *wishful-thinking* that ignores selected realities.

It is part of the challenge of accepting the world the way it is versus the *wishful-thinking* that supports notions of how one thinks the world ought to be. That is, what *ought-to-be* shaded by social and political values that may or may not be viable or desirable.

There is also an interpretation of SE that focuses on the truthfulness or falsity of held opinions. For example, there is generally more credence given to testimony from someone known or believed to have expertise in the chosen topic than someone who does not. That is, known competence adds credibility to a person's statements but only within their area of competence.[132]

On the other hand, advertising, of all types, often violates this notion of expert testimony through the use of individuals, who are famous or have credibility in some field, to make statements about subjects totally unconnected with their supposed area of fame or expertise.

In fact, advertisements, both political and commercial, are constantly making claims that appear, superficially, valid, but on closer examination are found to be fallacious. One of the most common errors they make, on purpose, are category mistakes, where there appears to be a connection, but none really exists. [see above *Explanations and Perception* - page 140]

In summary, the SE doctrine, essentially says that it is allowable to ignore or modify physical facts to meet social agendas. Put another way, this means that empirical or factual knowledge modified or filtered by social agendas, or even the use of counterfactual content, is acceptable practice.

Social Constructionism

Wikipedia Definition: "A social construct or construction concerns the meaning, notion, or connotation placed on an object or event by a society and adopted by the inhabitants of that society with respect to how they view or deal with the object or event. In that respect, a social construct as an idea would be widely accepted as natural by the society but may or may not represent a reality shared by those outside the society and would be an *invention or artifice of that society*."

---

[132] In the field of Information Technology there is an old insider joke, that an *expert* is someone from out of town.

2.2 Contemporary History

Social Constructionism (hereinafter SC) is an extension of SE that emphasizes the social and cultural aspects of human societies as opposed to hereditary or other physical aspects of humanity that, in general, defines human society, and, in particular, defines us as individuals.

SC advocates take the position that it is the social interactions that are of importance in the determination of our worldview and how we interpret our society and our place in society. Also, that these social interactions and conventions are valid only within the society that advocates and accepts these social practices.

Additionally, SC advocates believe that even the physical sciences are subjective. They claim that only a scientific fact that is a demonstrated universal can be accepted unconditionally, all else is tentatively held as provisionally valid. Since scientific theories are always subject to possible revision or even revocation, there is some truth to the claim that science is not fixed. However, this does not mean that true science is driven by social subjectivity or, at least, it should not be.

For example: In the history of astronomy, *facts* changed from geo-centric to helio-centric and from circular planetary orbits to elliptical orbits. This list could be extended with many examples where *scientific truths* were either discredited or modified to meet new speculations concerning how nature works. Also, recall the above comments about the electron.

It seems that, at least, a part of common (or naïve) reality is created from social interactions (events and objects), therefore, reality is not a completely objective truth but rather it is a point of view modified and influenced by the aims and beliefs of a particular society. [See *Types of Reality*, page 155]

According to its advocates, SC offers an alternative to the western intellectual tradition. For example, when they say gender is socially constructed, they usually mean that it is not the obvious biological differences that define gender so much as social traditions and historical influences that create and define gender as usually manifested. Or, do they mean that society wills a certain *gender* definition that forms our belief in stereotypical gender norms?[133]

---

[133] Anyone who has actually parented children from birth have all seen that there are certain characteristics that quickly differentiate gender in infants and toddlers well before any social influences could take effect.

Some, the more radical, claim that currently defined gender roles are harmful and wrong such that they need to be changed or even eliminated. This is a specific case of the more general notion held by constructionists that most of our beliefs are not inevitable but are merely social conventions that society has created. That is, it is a belief in ontological relativism.[134]

With regard to gender variability, I can only repeat a previous comment that no matter the cuts made by the topiary designer, the plant is still the same plant.

It is really not clear where these advocates of SC demarcate between what is socially constructed and what, if any, is ontic and objective in the sense of being a veridical truth. For example, SC, being in step with secular liberalism, claims that all morality is merely a human construction and that moral issues are only valid within the society that holds these values, and it is completely legitimate for another society to hold the opposite views.

Summary
One of the problems with the followers of SE and SC is that like other apostles of strongly held beliefs (left or right), they tend to take their position too far and are too inflexible.

Advocating the replacement of facts with socially motivated notions is, at least partially, a denial of reality and an attempt to seek solace in a world of fantasy. It is simply *wishful thinking* about the way they believe things should be, instead of what is actual, possible, or even desirable.

To make matters even worse, this is mostly done with little of no concern about the long-term implications and impact of their social agendas. That is, like so many other activists, they are only focused on the short-term impact of their actions, if even that. There seems little or no concern about long terms effects, unexpected effects, or the question of whether some action is worth doing.

Whether or not advocates fully believe in the tenets of SE, SE does provide excuses and opportunities to conveniently fabricate *facts* in order to promote their agendas.

---

[134] This is the notion of anti-realism, where words like *exists*, *truth*, and *fact* are questioned beyond the common-sense notions of these words. That is, relativistic interpretations determine a reality that is socially variable.

2.2 Contemporary History

SE, especially when extended by constructivism relieves them of any need to be rational, logical, or even truthful. This, of course, creates a situation where serious and sober debate has become all but impossible because there are no rational objections that the SE followers will accept.

To Summarize, the notions of SE, augmented with constructivism, denies most, if not all, epistemic knowledge as being factual, in the traditional meaning of knowledge. This allows them to conceive any convenient notion and declare that notion to be factual and even desirable. What long term impact all of this will have is, of course, impossible to know but from history, we do know that societies that decline morally (and this is an indicator of moral decline) will also decline or even cease to exist.

Revisionist History and Contextual Displacement

It is a normal and legitimate occupation of historians to use new discoveries and original research to reinterpret prior evidence and to modify previous analyses of historical events in order to augment and enhance our understanding of events in the past. However, it is not the role of historians to reinterpret the past using contemporary moral judgments or contemporary social agendas.

When someone who is not a historian considers what they believe is an historical fact, they commonly do so within the context of present day society and their own personal views. This constitutes a displacement of context from the social and personal conventions of the time when these events occurred into contemporary attitudes and opinions.

Although, presenting the past in current context is a common practice, for a non-historian to do so is careless and misleading but for a historian to do this is deceptive and fallacious.

History is full of injustices that caused many to suffering, but these events should be kept in their original context. To do otherwise is an injustice to those living today who are wrongly accused of perpetuating or in some way being culpable for events that occurred in the distant past.

That is, to condemn individuals or ethnic groups living today as being either responsible or complicit in some way for injustice that occurred before they were born and, in many cases, even hundreds of years in the past, is irrational, illogical, and a gross injustice.[135]

This practice of condemnation is found, either implicitly or explicitly, in revisionist history that emphasizes the negative and minimizes the positive. Some use the term *negationism* for this type of revision. That is, the positive and optimistic is downplayed or ignored while the negative and pessimistic is over emphasized.

Additionally, this type of negative history seems to target the US most often and with a degree of imbalance that leaves little room for objectivity.

---

[135] For example, this is like blaming the current British royal family for the excesses of their ancestors such as those of Henry VIII and his daughter Queen (Bloody) Mary.

2.2 Contemporary History

Unfortunately, this type of negative revisionism has found its way into many, if not most, educational systems in this country.[136]

Examples of condemnations, through contextual displacement are many but here are two examples that are especially active within society today. First, in the US, perhaps the most common injustice is the perpetuation of blame for slavery, and, second, is the European incursion into the western hemisphere and the subsequent subjugation of the western hemisphere's indigenous population by Europeans.

With regard to the first example, it should be remembered, that in the context of the past, slavery was as common as owning livestock, and essentially, at one time or another, just about every race and ethnic group on earth participated in slavery to some degree. Africans owned slaves, Amerindians owned slaves, Christians owned slaves, Muslims owned slaves, ancient Jews owned slaves, and so on.

Given the social mores of today's society, slavery of all types is rightly condemned as evil and inhumane, but in the past, essentially throughout the history of humanity, slavery was an economic issue with little or no thought given to morality or human rights.[137]

The second example is the condemnation of Europeans in general, and European men in particular for the occupation and subjugation of the Americas over the period from 1492 through the end of the 19th century. This 400-year process resulted in the political, ethnical, and social structures that now exist on the continents of the Americas and, as with all great human events, was a mixture of the good and the bad.[138]

However, among this multitude of political entities that exist on these continents, it is only the US that is condemned by certain activists as a corrupt and evil country, while, at the same time, it is this country where, it seems, many millions of people strongly desire to live.

---

[136] A prime example of negativists history and an unbalanced approach is the popular book by Howard Zinn, *A People's History of the United States*, Harper Collins, New York, 1980.

[137] That is, the acceptance of slavery was a social convention at the time and locations where it was practiced and, therefore, for an advocate of SC, within that society the practice of slavery moral and should not be condemned because we have a different sense of morality.

[138] The essays in Part 1 show that sometimes it is not possible to separate the good and the bad, and that which is deemed good or bad are different in different epochs.

I have not heard of millions of people wanting to migrate to Mexico or any other country in the western hemisphere, but millions have migrated, both legally and illegally, and still more millions want to migrate to this country that politically progressive elements finds so awful. I don't get it?!

To be sure, events in the past have influence on the present, but this is not the same as carrying forward the events of the past as a means for perpetuating prior grievances. Carrying forward the sins of the past provides invalid excuses for the continuation of past grievances.

It seems that, in this country, some live with one foot in the present and one in the past, such that they continue to ignore the many changes that have taken place in this country that has improved social relations to the point where a minority president was elected - twice!

Of course, all is not perfect, while the social imbalance that plagued the US for decades has been reduced for minorities, while for others, especially men, in general, and those of European descent, in particular, are increasingly being marginalized with regard to their ability to speak openly or candidly about sensitive social issues.

Honest historians approach the past with an open mind and refrain from judgments based on contemporary notions of right and wrong. The objective historian will present what is known along with interpretations that are consistent with the morals and attitudes of the period being discussed.

It is indeed unfortunately that far too often history is a revisionist effort that tends toward interpretations and judgements against standards that did not exist in the past. We see these revisionist historical interpretations most often when there exists strong political, religious, or other emotional issues that use what occurred in the past as an indicator, cause, or excuse for today's problems, real or imagined.

Some call revisionism a necessary and legitimate updating of historical content. This is true up to a certain point, but when revision is done not for scholastic reasons, such as new discoveries or legitimate reevaluation of historical artifacts, but for contemporary social and political agendas, revisionism becomes a false narrative.

Besides contextual displacement, there are other techniques that are used by revisionists to make alterations that comply with their chosen agendas. For example, logical fallacies, category mistakes, and just plain lying are

2.2 Contemporary History

often used. Inventiveness is certainly not lacking when it comes to negativism and contextual displacement.

One of the purposes of historical works is to understand the errors of the past but not to bring them forward with displaced context for purposes of placing blame on contemporaries or to replace one type of bias by another.

To displace historical context is not history, but propaganda. To be sure, as mentioned, there is sometimes a fine line between history and propaganda, but the honest historian will avoid crossing over into the domain propaganda.

Appendix A: Reconsidering Global Warming

Is Global Warming an Example of SE or SC?

Computer Simulations and Modeling

Computerized modeling has made its way into such diverse areas as weather forecasting, economics, and even political campaigns. But for all that, the non-technical person has no clue about how such modeling works or even whether it is reliable or not. The non-specialist stakeholder is unable to assess whether or not that model has built-in bias or even if the model actually *models* or is just a self-fulfilling prophesy. This, of course, is just one of the problems with models.

The simple truth is that all models are always a simplification of reality and, sometimes, these models are constructed by persons with social or personal agendas. Put simply, they may be merely self-serving tools designed to support a particular position.

Essentially, we are led to believe that models have a degree of accuracy sufficient for forecasting and that these models should be accepted as valid. The implication is that enough cause and effect is known about the subject matter such that the model is reliably accurate and should be accepted as valid.

That is, the basic assumption is that these models are designed to mimic actual phenomena with a degree of accuracy that conforms to some standard of usability and utility, which implies obtaining acceptable margins of error.

The model's usability and utility depend on the model having reasonably accurate predictive capabilities of the model. That is, the predictive accuracy depends on how many causal parameters are identified, understood, and properly coded, as well as, the initial conditions for the model all determine how well the algorithms mimic the actual processes being modeled.

Initial conditions, which specify the starting point for simulations, can be problematic because of constantly changing conditions, and incomplete or inaccurate data. We regularly see this problem with short range weather predictions, which are relatively simple when compared with the complexity of trying to forecast long term climate changes.

Appendix A

Additionally, these models often require extreme extrapolations that can easily introduce error. Such extrapolations are necessary because in complex modeling, not all parameters are known or properly understood as to either their collective interactions or their individual influence. Put simply, even the best models are only approximations of real conditions and need be viewed with an element of skepticism.

I can state from personal experience that in the development of computer models, it is common to use trial and error when *calibrating* or *fine-tuning* models. This is an iterative process where parameters are adjusted until the desired results are achieved or an acceptable margin of error is obtained when compared to test data that is supposed to be a real-world scenario. This technique is never completely satisfactory, because it requires adjusting for short-term effects while ignoring the more long-term effects.

Global Climate Discussion

There is no doubt that given its complexity, global climate is an example of a causally complex processes, where not all variables and parameters have been determined as to amount of influence or, indeed, have all variables even been identified. Modeling dozens of variables and parameters is only possible with great difficulty and, like all measurements, are only approximately accurate.

Another problem with forecasting long-term climate changes is the lack of complete empirical data that is consistently accurate and complete over the period of many decades or even centuries. Historically, the only thing recorded was temperature data, and that was limited to only a smattering of locations while there was no data at all for most of the planet.

Even as recently as 50 or 60 years ago, there were large geographical gaps where no or little weather information was available. For example, during the cold war, the former Soviet Union, withheld weather data that covered the largest contiguous land mass on earth, Siberia. Plus, weather data form the vast Pacific Ocean was scant, which meant that two of the most critical regions for weather sources were missing or incomplete.

Historically, we know that the temperatures in the Northern Hemisphere were colder about 800 or 900 years ago, and we know that, again, in the late medieval period and up to the early 19th century temperatures averaged lower than now.

For example, after nearly two centuries, ice festivals on the River Thames at London ceased in the early 19th century, because the Thames River no longer froze over. Other examples from the *Little Ice Age* over the last 1000 years or so include:

1133: The River Po, in northern Italy, became covered with ice from Cremona to the estuary.

1200+: Because of colder temperatures, Norse settlers in Greenland shifted from farming and livestock to fishing for food. As the climate continued to grow colder, eventually, all Norse settlements in Greenland had to be abandoned.

1234: The River Po was again frozen, as was the Rhone River in southern France.

1468: It was so cold, that soldiers in Flanders divided their wine supply with axes.

1635: The upper Rhine River froze at Speyer. (Severe winters, and subsequent famine that occurred in the first half of the 17th century, are seen as partial causes of the First Thirty Years War.)

1638: In southern France, the Marseilles harbor froze.

This, of course, is just a short list of the many instances that have indicated over the centuries that significant climate change is a continuous condition and is nothing new, nor is it necessarily a manmade phenomenon.

Although there does appear to be some trending toward a somewhat warmer climate there is, at this time, no comprehensive cause and effect evidence that can rationally be considered 100% conclusive.

The suspects are many, but the actual culprit or culprits have not been conclusively identified or implicated as to degree of influence. Everything from the popular carbon dioxide villain to the more exotic Gamma Ray villain has been accused, but conclusive evidence is just not there.

Another possibility that doesn't seem to get much attention are the so-called Milankovitch Cycles.[139] This is the name given to the conjecture that it is the combination of perturbations in the Earth's orbit that cause periods of both warming and cooling. These factors are *orbital precession, orbital eccentricity, axial tilt*, and *precession*. Together, these four factors represent a complex system of cycles within cycles where the cumulative effects are not completely identified.

---

[139] Named after Milutin Milanković (Serbian Polymath, 1879 – 1958)

Appendix A

The Milanković Cycles conjecture seems an extension of the *known causes* of seasonal climate changes to include long term cyclical effects on climate. Although not proven, it has plausibility and rates serious consideration.

Actual understanding of global climate is also hindered because this issue has become highly politicized and when this happens, we all know that rationality and facts become secondary to political agendas.

To be sure, determining the true cause is difficult enough without the confusion and misinformation caused by political polarization, which has progressed to such a degree that rational discussion is not possible.

Indeed, the verbal attacks of the true believers against skeptics has escalated to the point of being nothing more than personal insult, and a complete unwillingness to even listen to any voice of caution or skepticism.[140]

Although humans are part of nature, there appears little doubt, that human technology and population growth has reached the point of being a real test of nature's restorative and regenerative capabilities. Even so, environmental changes are so subtle and complex that complete understanding of cause and effect is not yet fully determined. Moreover, environmental changes are not smooth transitions, but proceed with the unevenness and complexity of cycles within cycles.

---

[140] For example, Mr. Bill Nye, a TV personality who claims to be a scientist, uses extremely abusive language to disparage anyone who disagrees with him. He consistently uses such catchy phrases as *anti-science, temple of lies* and *temple of ignorance* to name just a few. Such language is certainly not productive or the mark of a rational person. Of course, he isn't the only one to use such abusive and insulting language.

Selected Bibliography

Ambrose, Stephen. Crazy Horse and Custer. New York: Anchor Books, 1996.

de Madariaga, Salvador. Hernan Cortes: Conqueror of Mexico. Garden City, NY: Anchor Books, 1969

Diaz del Castillo, Bernal. The Discovery and Conquest of Mexico. Farrar, Straus, and Cudahy, 1956.

Fox, Richard. Archeology: History, and Custer's Last Stand. Norman: University of Oklahoma Press, 1993.

Graham, W. A. The Custer Myth: A Source Book of Custeriana. New York: Bonanza Books, 1953.

Gray, John S. Custer's Last Campaign. Lincoln: University of Nebraska Press, 1991.

The Holy Bible.

Kuhlman, Charles. Legend into History: The Custer Mystery. Harrisburg, PA: Telegraph Press, 1951.

Panzeri, Peter. Little Bighorn 1876: Custer's Last Stand. Oxford: Osprey Publishing, 1995.

Philbrick, Nathaniel. The Last Stand. New York: Penguin Group, 2010.

Thomas, Hugh. Conquest: Montezuma, Cortes, and the Fall of Old Mexico. NY, NY: Simon and Shuster, 1993

The Quran.

General Index

Abbasid Caliphates, 23
Abbasids, 23
Abraham, 15, 16, 24
accommodation: dynamic, 149
Aisha, 18
Albigensian, 50
Alexander VI: Pope, 49
Al-Malik: Abd, 22
Amerindians, 47, 48, 176
Apostles, 6, 7, 8, 10
Apostolic Period, 6, 11, 12
Arabia, 15, 16, 17, 19, 24
Aragon, Kingdom of, 32
Army: US, 62, 90
Austria-Hungary, 100, 109, 112
Bahira, 16
Bakr: Abu, 19
Battle of Badr, 17
Bedouin, 17, 24
belief: sufficient evidence for, 136
Benteen, Frederick, 61, 69, 73-75, 74, 76-80, 78, 79, 81-89, 88, 93
Bernal Diaz, 31, 39, 43
Bible, 10, 136
Borgia, Cesare, 49
Bosnian, 50
Breitenfeld: Battle of, 55
Byzantine Empire, 20
Calhoun Hill, 83
Caliph, 19, 20, 21, 22, 23
Callixtus III: Pope, 49
Castile, Kingdom of, 32
Catholic Church, 12, 26, 32, 142
Catholic League, 54, 55
Catholics, 55
cause: and effect, 148
Cheyenne, 62, 80
China, 115, 125
Cholula, 34, 35
Christianity, 3-13, 16, 24, 26, 27, 28, 47, 51
City: of the Prophet, 17
Civil War, 63, 65

Clemenceau: French Prime Minister, 109
clock, 141
conceptual displacement, 175
Constantinople, 12, 13, 20, 28, 49, 142
Cooke: Custer's Adjutant, 75, 76
Cortes, Hernan, 33, 34, 35, 36, 37, 38, 39, 40, 41, 42, 47, 183
Crazy Horse, 63
Crook, General George, 66, 67, 68, 69
Crow's Nest, 71, 72, 73
Cuauhtémoc, 40, 45
Cuba, 29, 33, 35, 36
Custer Hill, 83, 88
Custer Ridge, 83
Custer, battle area, 80
Custer, George Armstrong, 62, 63, 64, 66, 68, 69, 75, 76, 83, 87, 88, 89, 91, 93, 94, 95, 96
Dakota Territory, 66
de Alvarado: Pedro, 29, 37
de Borja: Alfons, 49
de Cuéllar: Diego Velázquez, 29, 33
Deep Ravine, 83
Defenestration: of Prague, 53
d'Espagnat, Bernard, 148
Displacement, Contextual, 175
electron, 170
English, 46, 47, 142
Entente Cordial, 99
Ephesus, 10
Epistemology: Social, 169
explanations, 140
Ford A, 75, 76
France, 12, 22, 51, 54, 56, 58, 181
Frederick, the Great, 97
French, 46, 47, 56
Gabriel: Archangel, 16
German, 51, 53, 55, 58
German, reparations, 111, 113
Germany, 99-103, 99, 100, 108-14, 117-21, 124

184

Gibbon, Col. John, 66, 68, 91
Global Warming, 179
Gödel, Kurt, 166
Godfrey, Lt, 70
Granada, 32, 41
groupthink, 150
Gustavus Adolphus: King of Sweden, 55
Hashemite, 15, 20, 25
Hegira, 17
Hispaniola, 39
History, Revisionist, 175
Hitler: Adolf, 114, 116, 117, 122, 124
Hussein, 21
Hussite: Wars, 26, 50, 53
Information: Deprivation, 161
Injustice: Epistemic or Testimonial, 164
intersubjective agreement, 149
Iran, 19, 21, 25
Iraq, 19, 21
Islam, 3, 4, 15, 17–23, 22, 24–28, 41, 49
Japan, 111, 125
Jerusalem, 6, 9, 11, 12, 22, 27, 28; Council of, 7
Jesus, 5, 6, 8, 16, 25
Jewish, 5, 6, 7, 8, 9, 10, 15, 17
Jordan, 19, 25
judgments, 30, 135, 136, 137, 177; hasty and otherwise, 135
Kaaba, 15, 18
Keynes, John Maynard, 108
knowledge, intimate, 142
knowledge, symbolic, 142
language, 139
Leighton, J. A., 154
light, 144
Little Bighorn River, 68, 71, 74, 84, 87
Lubeck: Treaty of, 55
Lutzen: Battle of, 55
Manchurian Incident, 115
Martin, John, 77, 78, 81, 82
martyrdom, 5
Marwan II: Caliph, 23
Matthew, 5
Mecca, 15, 16, 17, 18, 19, 22, 26

media: social, 146, 159, 160, 162
Medicine Tail Coulee, 81
Medina, 17, 18, 22, 26
Mexica, 31, 32, 33, 34, 36, 38, 39, 40, 41, 42, 43, 44, 45
Mexican, 29, 31, 32, 33, 36, 38, 40, 42, 43, 44
Mexicans, 31, 38, 39, 44, 45
Mexico, 29, 30, 31, 33, 34, 40, 41, 45, 47, 177, 183
Milankovitch Cycles, 181
Models: Computer, 179
Montezuma, 29, 31, 33, 34, 35, 36, 37, 38
Moses, 16, 25
MTC, Medicine Tail Coulee, 81, 82, 87
Muawiyah, 22
Muhammad, 15, 16, 17, 18, 19, 20, 22, 24, 25, 26
Narvaez', 39
National Socialism, 114
Nazi, 114, 116, 165
Netherlands: Spanish, 51
Nicene Creed, 12, 142
Nine Beatitudes, 5
Nordlingen: First Battle of, 55
Nye-Cartwright Ridge, 82
Orthodox Church, 12, 142
Orthodoxy: Eastern, 13, 142
Ottoman Turks, 23
Ottomans, 28, 54
pack train, 73, 74, 76, 77, 78, 79, 81, 82, 83, 86, 87, 88
Paris Peace Conference, 108
Paul of Tarsus, 7
perception: sensitivity of, 145
Persians, 23, 28
Peter and Paul, 8, 9
Pollution: Sensory, 143
Prague, 53, 54, 55, 56
Protestant League, 53
Protestants, 27, 47, 53, 54, 55
Prussia, 97, 102
Quran, 20, 26
Quraysh tribe, 15, 20, 22
Rashidun Caliphs, 19, 23

reality: reconsidered, 154; types of, 155; *versus actual*, 154
Reformation, 13, 26, 27, 50, 51; The, 27
religion, 137, 138
Renaissance, 49, 50
Reno, 88
Reno, Creek, 74, 75
Reno, Hill, 77, 78, 79, 82, 83, 84, 86, 87, 88
Reno, Major Marcus, 61, 69, 72–80, 81–89, 91, 93
reparation, 114
resurrection, 5
Rhineland, 108
Roman Empire, 6, 8, 13, 20, 26
Rome, 8, 9, 11, 12, 13, 19, 41, 49, 51
Rosebud, 66, 67, 68, 69, 70, 71, 86, 91
Royce, Josiah, 143
Sarajevo, 100
Sasanian, 19
Saud: House of, 25
Saudi Arabia, 25
Scandinavia, 50
second revolt: of the Jews, 11
sensory pollution, 144
Serbia, 100
Sermon on the Mount, 5
Sheridan: General Phillip, 66, 67
Shia, 21, 23
Sioux, 66, 67, 69–77, 80, 81, 84, 88, 89
slavery, 176
Somme, The Battle of the, 103
South Skirmish Line, 83
Soviet, 118, 121, 123, 180
Spain, 33, 34, 41, 42, 51, 56
Spanish, 29, 31, 32, 34, 35, 37–47, 51, 54, 56, 90, 161
Syria, 8, 15, 16, 19, 20
Talib: Abi, 19
Tarsus, 7
technology: too much, 145
Tenochtitlan, 31, 34, 35, 36, 37, 38, 39, 40, 43, 44, 45
Terry, General Alfred, 66, 68, 69, 71, 85, 88
Tlaxcala, 31, 34, 38, 39
Tlaxcalan, 36
Tours: Battle of, 22
Treaty of Versailles, 108
truth: about, 152
Tyranny: of Imposition, 166
Umar, 19, 20
Umayyad Caliphs, 22, 23
Umayyad Dynasty, 22, 23
Unexpected: The, 147, 167
US First Army, 107
USA, 64, 105, 135, 139, 161
Uthman, 20, 21, 22
Varnum, Charles, 71
Verdun, The Battle for, 103
Villa Rica, 33, 34, 36, 39
War: Thirty Years, 56
Warriors, numbers of, 75
Washita, 62, 63, 69, 87
Weimar Republic, 110, 113
Weir Point, 77, 79, 81, 82, 83
Weir, Captain Thomas, 77, 79, 83
Westphalia: Peace of, 56
White Mountain: Battle of, 54
Wilson: Woodrow, 109, 110
World War II, 115, 135
worldview, 157
Yemen, 15, 16

Made in the USA
San Bernardino, CA
06 May 2018